William Tatlock

The Revelation of God in Christ and Other Sermons

Preached at St. John's Church, Stamford, Conn.

William Tatlock

The Revelation of God in Christ and Other Sermons
Preached at St. John's Church, Stamford, Conn.

ISBN/EAN: 9783337114459

Printed in Europe, USA, Canada, Australia, Japan

Cover: Foto ©Lupo / pixelio.de

More available books at **www.hansebooks.com**

SERMONS

BY

WILLIAM TATLOCK,

PRIEST AND DOCTOR.

THE REVELATION OF GOD IN CHRIST AND OTHER SERMONS, PREACHED AT ST. JOHN'S CHURCH, STAMFORD, CONNECTICUT, BY THE LATE REVEREND WILLIAM TATLOCK, D. D., RECTOR.

NEW YORK, JAMES POTT & CO.,
PUBLISHERS, FOURTH AVENUE
AND TWENTY-SECOND STREET
A. D. 1897.

✠

Messrs. James Pott & Co.

MIDDLETOWN, CONN., March 18, 1897.

MY DEAR SIRS:

Were I asked to characterize in two words my opinion of the late DR. TATLOCK AS A PREACHER, I should say that he *was always* in the best sense of the words, *spiritual and edifying*. He was never sensational; his intellectual and moral character forbade anything of the sort. I am sure, however, that his sermons never lacked what used to be called unction, and that it was their own fault if his hearers did not carry away from them the best lessons in the Christian faith and for the Christian life.

I am glad to know that you propose to issue a volume of his sermons, and am sure it will be welcomed by our whole Church.

Sincerely yours,
J. WILLIAMS,
Bishop of Connecticut.

NEW YORK, March 17, 1897.

GENTLEMEN:

A wide circle of readers, I cannot but think, will welcome a volume of Twenty Sermons by Dr. William Tatlock, whose well furnished mind, clear vision, and firm grasp of the truth, made him a teacher eminently fitted to be helpful and stimulating to his generation.

Sincerely yours,
H. C. POTTER,
Bishop of New York.

DEAR SIRS: I rejoice to know you are to publish a volume of sermons by Dr. William Tatlock, of St. John's Parish, Stamford. I held him in high esteem for his great ability and rare devotion to the cause of the Church and her mission in this country, in which he held a conspicuous position, both in his diocese and in the Church at large.

Yours truly,
ETHELBERT TALBOT,
Bishop of Wyoming, etc.

March 18, '97.

THE REVELATION OF GOD
IN CHRIST.

CHRISTMAS DAY, S. JOHN'S, STAMFORD, DECEMBER 25, 1891.

THE REVELATION OF GOD IN CHRIST.

"God, who at sundry times and in divers manners spake in time past unto the fathers by the prophets, hath in these last days spoken unto us by His Son."—HEBREWS i. 2.

In the Old Testament, as in the New, God reveals Himself. But in the former He reveals Himself in history and prophecy, and the revelation is fragmentary and incomplete, proportioned in growing measures to growing capacities —"the Law was a schoolmaster," and the processes were educational.

In the New Testament He reveals Himself through the Incarnation of the Word—as the spoken word expresses the inward thought, so the Word of God reveals God. "In these last days He hath spoken unto us by His Son—a revelation perfect to our present understanding, and which grows fuller as we can more fully take it in. Jesus Christ is the Only-begotten of the Father, full of grace and truth."

In the New Testament, therefore, religion takes on its form as distinctively *the Christian religion—God revealed in Christ.* What *is* the Christian religion?

It is, *that adhesion of the soul which we call faith, to a person, Jesus Christ, who is Himself very God, and who took upon Himself our human nature, and became very Man, "for us and for our salvation."* And by salvation we understand deliverance from the sin of which human nature is conscious, and the restoration and perfection in us of that image of God in which we were created, so that our life, beginning here and extended through eternity, may be a conscious life of holiness and its consequent blessedness. This is the Christmas Gospel—the good news to the race of man.

The Founder of Christianity has taught the final deliverance of the personal man from all evil and his eternal personal existence in satisfying communion with God. And in order to this, such a personal relation and adhesion to Himself as a Divine Being, as carries with it personal love, and free obedience, and submission in all things to the Divine will. And this because He is true God, and in the relation of the human soul to Him is life—a true moral and spiritual life. The Deity is revealed to men in the Incarnate Christ. "No man hath seen God at any time; the Only-begotten Son, which is in the bosom of the Father, He hath declared Him." The Incarnation is the final word, the complete revelation of God, *so far as we can take it in.* We take it in more and more largely and adequately as we cultivate religion and grow in the spiritual life. Never completely, in this present stage of our existence, "Now we see through a glass darkly, but then face to face; now we know in part, but then shall we know, even as also we are known." But, in our measure, according to our capacity, we *do* know, we *take it in*, we apprehend God as He is revealed in Jesus Christ. The Christian religion is the soul's conscious acceptance of, and adhesion to, the Personal, Divine Christ manifested in human form and substance—one with ourselves, yet one with God, the one mediator between God and man.

As we read in the Gospels the statement and story of the Incarnation, and set out to think about it, we are staggered by the conception of an event so unprecedented, so unique, so utterly supernatural. The most devout believer, as he dwells upon it, finds it hard to take it in. And indeed a man is not an unbeliever and a heretic because he cannot easily organize his thought of God Incarnate. It is the most tremendous conception that can be presented to the human mind; and, as I shall have occasion to say further on, the conditions under which the average man thinks are not favorable to conceptions of anything so unprecedented, so entirely supernatural.

But, notwithstanding, it is as possible to take in the thought of God in the image of man, as it is to take in the thought of man in the image of God. What is it that we mean by that expression? It is, *that a man is a spiritual being enshrined in a material one.* The manner of it human thought is inadequate to conceive, and human language is inadequate to tell. Who can describe the soul's connection with the body? Who can tell what life is? And what is death? We talk of the difficulty of conceiving the supernatural. Do we always find it easy to describe adequately what we call the natural? Because a thing is familiar, has happened before, we call it natural; and we call that supernatural which is unprecedented. But indeed the natural is ever emerging out of the supernatural. The bounds of the supernatural are receding and the bounds of the natural are advancing and enlarging as the race grows in intelligence. Take what theory we will of the evolution of the world, new things have happened, new forms have appeared, new forces have been manifested, which, in relation to the order of nature as previously understood, were supernatural happenings. They were supernatural until they had appeared, and then they became natural. To God all things are natural, and when we fully comprehend the order of nature they will be natural to us. And one day we shall comprehend it.

On this principle we can account for the Incarnation. There is a close relation between man and his Maker. They are alike in their qualities of personality, intelligence, will, and affection. It is the natural thing that they should know each other. The Father and His children were not intended to be strangers and apart. How shall they come to know each other? And to love each other? This is the question that is answered by the Incarnation. Man cannot of himself find out God. God must find man. *He has found him.* Man can know Him Who made him in His own image, can recognize the Father of his spirit, can know Him for worship, duty, and love. The moral order of the world is complete. The Divine purpose is rounded out in fulfilment. However difficult it may be to conceive of the Personal Creator making Himself known to His personal and intelligent creatures, it is still more difficult to conceive of His not doing so. That would mean an unintelligible world.

How has He done it? And how could He have done it better?

There are three ways conceivable in which men might acquire some practical knowledge of God. The first is, by a series of statements, or propositions, giving information about Him. The second is, by His exhibiting Himself in action—from what He does we may learn a great deal about the Doer. The third is, by manifesting Himself in Person, so that men see Him, hear Him, live with Him, get into touch with Him.

1. Some idea of God might conceivably be obtained through description of His attributes and qualities. To illustrate this, let me quote from Chapter II., of the Westminster Confession of Faith : "There is but one only living and true

God, who is infinite in Being and Perfection, a most pure Spirit, Invisible, without Body, Parts or Passions, Immutable, Immense, Eternal, Incomprehensible, most Wise, most Holy, most Free, most Absolute, working all things according to the counsel of his own Immutable and most Righteous Will, for his own Glory, most Loving, Gracious, Merciful, Long-suffering, abundant in Goodness and Faith, forgiving Iniquity, Transgression and Sin, the rewarder of them that diligently seek him, and withal, most just and terrible in his Judgment, hating all sin, and who will by no means clear the Guilty." Now here is a description of the Supreme Being by an enumeration of His attributes and qualities, a series of propositions about God, and there is a text of Scripture appended to each proposition, to prove it. They are all true. We can understand what it is all meant to teach, because the men who framed it had obtained their ideas from the Bible, and we have read the Bible. It is intelligible to educated people, who understand the meaning of words derived from the Latin. It is not interesting, but it is intelligible. But suppose this description of the Supreme Being to be set before one who had never read the Bible, nor taken in from his environment any Bible ideas. What would these propositions teach him about God? What sort of working idea of God would be given him? What foundation would be here on which to construct a relation between himself and his Maker, involving worship, duty, and personal love? It requires a college education even to understand the terms of the description. And the majority of poor sinners have not had a college education. Even if man *could* understand God by description, human language is not adequate to describe Him to the mass of mankind. And God does not want to be known only by cultivated people.

2. But again, it is possible to learn much of God's character if we study His ways of dealing with men. He may manifest Himself in action. He has done this, and we have the record of how He has dealt with men, in the Old Testament. Plainly, this is not only more interesting, but also more intelligible. It is within the comprehension, sufficiently, of the average man. The Old Testament is, as we lately saw, a revelation of the true inwardness of history—the causes and consequences of things, the purpose and motive of them, are laid bare before our eyes. The principles on which God governs the world are made evident to us, and we feel that we know more of the world's Governor from the Old Testament history than we could have learned from any amount of description.

3. Infinitely beyond this, in interest and adequacy for the purpose, is the revelation which we have of God in Christ, as recorded in the story of the human life of Jesus which is told us in the Gospels. There is no narrative in the whole

THE REVELATION OF GOD IN CHRIST.

range of literature so graphic, so picturesque, so simple. No biography extant so perfectly reveals the man. From His birth to His ascension the lifelike image of Jesus is before us. He goes through experiences ordinary and extraordinary, and we follow Him. The most unlettered peasant reads his Bible, and sees Jesus living and moving in his very sight. And "he that hath seen Me," He says, "hath seen the Father." Such as the man Christ Jesus was, in the essentials of character, such is the Almighty Maker of heaven and earth. And is there anything which our moral sense could wish otherwise? He showed the best that man can be. Is it anything other than—to speak with reverence—other than God should be?

And how do we get this revelation? He never described Himself. He called twelve men around Him—twelve plain and honest men. They had no ends to serve in following Him, but His personality impressed them, and they followed Him. In utter simplicity and commonness of life they companied with Him, went in and out with Him as "He went about doing good." He was a Man among men, and for a time they thought of nothing beyond that. I doubt not it was an utter surprise to Peter himself when the Master's question, "Whom say ye that I am?" brought to a sudden point his frequent ponderings on the marvellous perfectness of the life with which he had bound up his

THE REVELATION OF GOD IN CHRIST.

own, and the confession burst forth incontinently, "Thou art the Christ, the Son of the living God." He could say nothing else.

I do not think we sufficiently appreciate that it was mainly the sustained and perfect *character* of Jesus that so impressed His immediate disciples—*His personality*. He grew upon them. He gave them no information out of His omniscience. He told them nothing about the other world, except that righteousness is the moral basis of things there as here. His miracles of themselves did not prove Him Son of God. His sinlessness, His utter unconsciousness of the evil that other men were conscious of, proved Him to be more than man. "They knew holiness when they saw it, and they saw that He was holy." There was only one way of explaining that—He *was* more than man. A perfectly holy being is Divine. He bound them, in an absolute trust and confidence, to His Person. It was not what He said. It was not what He did. It was *Himself*.

And when they came to write their recollections, it was *of Him* they wrote—His sayings and doings only picture Him. He taught, indeed, but "as one having authority." He had power. The writers of the Gospels are not making an argument. They are simply telling a story, and the story makes its own impression—the more effectively because it is so simply told. And it is worthy of note that though there is argument in the Epistles, it is not addressed to any point which is raised to-day. There is no discussion of "evidences." The opponents of Christianity then did not question the supernatural, nor doubt that Messiah could and would appear; they only denied that Jesus was the Messiah. They controverted Christianity from a Jewish, which was a religious point of view. With us it is Christ or nothing, and so we are concerned with the story of the Person of Christ, and that is distinctly told. It is the flavor of His personality that we catch throughout the Gospels and Epistles. Personal love and loyalty inspire them. And this it is, transmitted by the disciples in their subsequent intercourse with those whom they made Christians, and in their writings to us, that makes Christians in all times. The Christian religion is the conscious adhesion of the soul to the Person of Christ, Human and Divine. "This is life eternal, to know Thee, the only true God, and Jesus Christ, whom Thou hast sent."

The story of Jesus Christ, as given in the Gospels, is the most certain fact of history. There is more doubt about the existence of Napoleon Bonaparte than about the historic Christ. I am far from affirming that there is of necessity any intellectual dishonesty in unbelief, but it is an intellectual phenomenon, born of the assumption which controls many minds, that the supernatural is impossible—Jesus Christ cannot be, there-

THE REVELATION OF GOD IN CHRIST.

fore He is not. Rather, on irrefragable historic evidence, Jesus Christ is, therefore He can be.

And if Christ be a fact in the world's history, then you have to reckon with Him. He challenges you as certainly as your own existence challenges you. You cannot get away from it, nor from Him. What will you do with Him? What are you doing with Him? You may even wish that He had not come, but—*He is here.*

What hinders us to receive this Christmas Gospel? Why do men stick at the supernaturalness of the Incarnation—as if such an event could be anything other than supernatural! The question is rather, is there sufficient testimony? And is there an adequate purpose for it? And surely it is a sufficient purpose that God and man should be brought together—sufficient to explain any method God might make use of to accomplish such a reunion.

What slaves we are to the natural and the common! How fast bound by our environment, which is not favorable to the convictions, inspirations, and aspirations of the soul! How tied down to earth and its common ways!

The materialistic habit of mind is *the* difficulty in the way of apprehending God. He seems so unreal, or at least so vague, so far off, to us, because we are so occupied with material things and interests. But can any one suppose this materialistic habit of mind to be our normal condition?

What is there in the pursuits of men engrossed, as they confess, in business, to qualify them to pass judgment on the methods God takes to manifest Himself to mankind as a Being whom they should worship, and obey, and trust, and love? If there were no Sundays and no Church, what utter materialists we should all become!

I recently heard of a man, eminent in scientific pursuits, who replied to some question about religion, that he did not take the attitude of an unbeliever; he simply had not time to look into matters of that sort; he was absorbed in his other pursuits. And Mr. Darwin confesses that in the course of his eager study of a certain line of natural phenomena, he was conscious that his brain had gotten into a sort of atrophy as respects various intellectual interests which once were very much to him, and adds that "the loss of those tastes is a loss of happiness, and may possibly be injurious to the intellect, and more probably to the moral character, by enfeebling the emotional part of our nature."

If one of the great high priests of nature can make this confession as to the narrowing influence of scientific pursuits, with how much more reason may men feel that undue absorption in business life, with its admitted tendency to sordidness, to low ideals, to immoral methods and principles, explains the indisposition they feel to consider the supernatural aspects of religion, which is nothing if not supernatural. The aptitude for religion may become atrophied. It will, if it is not cultivated. Religion is intended to be a *cultus*. Life in the Church, simultaneously with life in the world, is God's provision for keeping the spiritual aptitudes in vigor.

Therefore the Church has instituted her order of the Christian year, that the round of supernatural facts, authentically recorded in the Scriptures, may be presented for our minds to dwell upon. The Incarnation of the Divine Son is one of these fundamental facts of religion. Christianity is faith in the human and Divine Christ. He is the Revealer of our God, who "in these last days hath spoken unto us by His Son." He is the final Word of God to men—the perfect manifestation. Human nature, indeed, still apprehends this perfect Word imperfectly, fragmentarily, according to the variously developed spiritual capacities of various men. But in various ways, and by degrees, *millions on millions of men have come to apprehend Him*, to know Him, to take Him in. And we shall know God better, if we want to know Him, *as He is in Christ, the Incarnate Word,* than in any other way conceivable to human thought.

The Christmas Gospel is that "the Word was made flesh, and dwelt among us, and we beheld His glory, the glory as of the Only-begotten of the Father, full of grace and truth."

THE REVELATION OF GOD IN THE OLD TESTAMENT SCRIPTURES.

SECOND SUNDAY IN ADVENT, S. JOHN'S, STAMFORD, DECEMBER 13, 1891.

THE REVELATION OF GOD IN THE OLD TESTAMENT SCRIPTURES.

"God, . . . at sundry times and in divers manners, spake in time past unto the fathers by the prophets."
—HEBREWS i. 1.

There can be no mistaking the meaning of the writer of this passage when he says that "God spake in time past to the fathers by the prophets." He refers to what we know as the revelation of God in the "Old Testament." He goes on to say that "in these last days God hath spoken unto us by His Son." Plainly he here refers to what we know as God's revelation of Himself in Jesus Christ, the record of which we have in the New Testament. His purpose in comparing the two revelations is to indicate the superiority of the later. And that justifies us in speaking of the Old Testament as inferior—considered as a means of making God known to man—inferior to the New. We all feel, somehow, that it is inferior, and the sacred writers saying so shows that we, too, may say so without irreverence. He gives the reasons for this inferiority: (1) The revelation in one case was through human agents, in the other by a Divine. (2) The earlier revelations were fragmentary, "at sundry times and in divers manners," literally, in separate portions and by distinct methods; there was never a final word; but the later was one full revelation—"in His Son"—a perfect and final expression of the Divine character. Nevertheless, though inferior, the Old Testament is still a Divine revelation. "*God spake* unto the fathers."

Consider to-day, therefore, the manner of revelation of the Divine character, purpose, will, as we have it in the Old Testament—"God, at sundry times and in divers manners, spake in time past unto the fathers by the prophets."

But why "at sundry times and in divers manners"? Why not at once a final word? Why was the earlier revelation fragmentary, and therefore at any one time imperfect? Why "in divers manners," so that any one method covered only a part of the ground? The answer is, because those to whom the successive revelations were made were *in a process of education.* Religious truth was taught them by degrees, "as they were able to bear it"—to take it in. Revelation is not an evolution, but the human capacity for receiving it is. It was then the childhood of the race. The perfect manhood of humanity is in Christ. He is the ideal, the representative, the pattern man. To remember this is essential to forming a true conception of the Old Testament Scriptures.

1. Of all the books that ever were written, the Bible stands alone in this, *that its purpose is to*

reveal God to man. And in connection with this, to teach man his true relation to his God, and, as a consequence, his true relation to his fellow-man.

We are met at the outset by the claim, made in the interest of what is now called agnosticism, that it is impossible for man to know God. "Canst thou by searching find God?" is asked. But that is not the question really pertinent to the case; it is a begging of the real question. The real question is, "Can God make Himself known to man?" Not, "Can man find God?" but "Can God find man?" Is there any way in which the intelligent Creator can sufficiently make Himself known to His intelligent creature? He Who made everything else, can He not make a revelation? There is force in agnosticism to this extent, that man cannot comprehend God *perfectly*, because a finite being cannot *comprehend* an Infinite. We cannot know God scientifically, adequately for the purpose of *knowing*; but we can know Him practically, adequately for the purpose of *doing*. We cannot define Him, but we can obey Him. Can a child define a parent? Yet he can obey him. And he can love him. And for that matter I do not know of any science in which men have yet got to the bottom of things. It is all, as yet, provisional and practical—mainly a working hypothesis; and I do not know why any more than this should be expected in theology, which is the science of religion. We *can apprehend* God, can know Him *sufficiently*, for certain purposes of mutual relation and intercourse. Such relation and intercourse between man and His Maker it is inconceivable that our Maker should not desire. We believe He does desire it. And so He has planned for it, has revealed enough of Himself to form a basis for intelligent *ap*prehension—not *com*prehension—and for spiritual intercourse, for duty and for love. He is not a lonely Being—childless. And we are not fatherless. The Bible teaches much of what God really is, and much more of what man really is, and of the relation between them. And in this the Bible stands alone as a *revelation*. What a different thing the world, life, man, would be without the revelation of God which it contains.

And what is it that, according to the universal interpretation of its teachings, the Bible reveals to us about God ? As to His nature, that He is a Spirit; as to His history, that He is Eternal; as to His character, that He is Good; as to His relation to the world, which is the practical use of a revelation, that He made it, preserves it, orders it, on principles of justice and benevolence.

What does it teach us about man ? As to his origin, that he is created by God. As to his nature, that he is in the image of Him that created him—has a spiritual nature. As to his character, that he is a moral being, having both good and evil tendencies, spiritual and animal, and is free to develop them in conduct. As to his future, that he has an unending existence, the character of which is determined by his character.

These are the primary truths of revelation. They are the basis of intelligent life and conduct. They are what our children first begin to enquire about, and what they need to learn as the alphabet of spiritual and moral training. They are the foundations of duty. And they are what the human race needed to be taught in its childhood, and what it can never outgrow. They are principles, to be developed and applied as the life of the race and the life of the individual go on. This teaching as to man's past and future explains his present. The thing every one of us needs to know, in order that we may live intelligently, is, *what God's purpose was in putting us into the world.* Then, we can go on to fulfil it, and make our lives a success—make them, *i.e., to answer the purpose.* Knowing God's relation to us, and our relation to Him, we know what is our duty toward God, and so what is our duty toward our neighbor.

Now, how this could have been better taught in the childhood of the race than as it was taught in the continuous process of education recorded in the Old Testament it is difficult to conceive. The Bible is the history of man's relation to God. And a religion that has no history is unsuited to a being who has a place in history. It is not reasonable that every man as he comes into the world should be required to construct his religion. He has not to construct his relations with his family. Nor yet to construct his relations with society. Neither should he be expected to construct his relations with his God. All these have their history, their traditions, their settled basis in facts, their first *rationale* in the general acceptance of Christendom. For it is not irrational to take for granted that *mankind* is more likely to be right than any *man* is. All the individual can do is to accept or reject these relations, to modify and improve them, but always to recognize them as facts and factors in his intelligent life.

The Bible is the only book which even professes to give, originally, the record of an historical religion from the first. In its pages we watch the development of man's relations with his God, and from a point of view which enables us to see at once both the Divine and the human points of view. It records the history, first of the race, and then of a selected people and of representative men. No matter that it does this often in poetic form, as the epic of human life—no matter that it embodies national traditions not to be interpreted as strictly and prosaically historical. Taken as a whole it presents a picture, a panorama of history and life, which makes a true and adequate impression upon us of the essential things we need to know in order to intelligently live in our own present. It gives us the *modus vivendi* between God and man. We stand off, as it were at a distance, to get the perspective, looking at Noah and the older world, at Abraham, Isaac and Jacob in their personal lives and as founding a nation, at Israel's national experiences and development, at Saul and David and Solomon in their temptations, struggles, sins and righteousnesses—and all the while we see God looking on, and helping and judging, as men are painfully working out their characters and life experiences. History is wrought out before our eyes from a point of view absolutely unique. We are behind the scenes—the judgment of a perfect Being on the passing things of earth and time is always before us. And in this way we learn that "the judgments of the Lord are true and righteous altogether." We see, therefore, things as they really were, not as they seemed at the time to be. Our vision is corrected, is achromatic, the white light of truth is poured upon them. And from what we learn of how God regarded those people and their various beings, doings, and sufferings, we know how He is to-day regarding us and ours. We see the wrong they did as *sin*, and the right they did as *righteousness*, and so we know what things are sins and what things are righteous, when we do them and when our neighbors do them, and when nations do them, even in this nineteenth century. Responsible beings are acting their parts all along, before the eyes of Him to Whom they are responsible, and our eyes take in the whole thing, the inner history, the actual relations. God's view of man's conduct and character, which is the true and lasting view, is set forth to us in the Scriptures.

This is strikingly illustrated in the national history recorded in the Old Testament. What a difference there is between the course of Hebrew history, as we have it there, and the course of, say Egyptian or Assyrian history, as we have it in their monuments. Throughout the Bible the point of view is the conformity, or non-conformity, of the nation's conduct to the will and law of God. That is the standard, always. In the other ancient histories, as recorded on their tablets, the will of a man—the king—is evidently the standard.* The Hebrews seem to be the only ancient people who recognized anything superior to the will of the king. They had what

---

* "The heathen nations had no corporate life, and seemed to exist only for the sake of swelling the pride and feeding the rapacity of the fierce monarchs at their head." "But Israel, as a civil community, presented a very different sight. . . . The government was a declared *theocracy*, exalting God and keeping down man. It was a free community which existed for the good of all its members; this was a striking contrast to every other national constitution in the world. Its laws, though defective upon a modern Christian standard, maintained justice and human rights. They involved the great principle of public good as the end and object of the state, in distinction from human greatness and power."—Mosby, Ruling Ideas, pp. 129, 130.

served the purpose of a constitution—there was something back of the ruler. Righteousness was not a human *dictum*, but a Divine law.

Again, and as a consequence, the Hebrew history freely narrates the faults and failures of its heroes, if heroes they can be called. It is true to life and facts. But what Assyrian tablet do we find that speaks of the faults, or even the failures, of the king? His conquests, his glory, his grandeur, his strength—never his goodness or badness—are the theme. You would never know that he was a being with moral character—only that he had a will and was strong to enforce it. He writes his own history, from his own point of view. What he does not like in his history we have to learn from his enemies. Pharaoh records his own triumphs—his defeats we learn from the Assyrian monuments. Neither of them speak of justice and mercy—the moral qualities of a king. These come into view when they touch the Hebrew history. Nebuchadnezzar, Belshazzar, Darius, Artaxerxes—their moral quality, the essential man, is brought out by Isaiah and Daniel. But in the Hebrew history these moral qualities of kings and peoples are the prominent things on the face of the record—it is written to show how God regarded kings and peoples. Only there do we see that "righteousness exalteth a nation, but sin is a reproach to any people." Profane history is the rankest materialism. Scripture history, throughout, is the history of morals and religion.

And this throws light on what we call the inspiration of the writers of the Old Testament. They were lifted up, from merely human and earthly points of view, to look at things from a point of view heavenly and Divine. They were taught to look at events as God looks at them, and so to record them. They spoke for Him, enabled by His Spirit. They were guided, taught, strengthened to be His prophets. They uttered His thoughts of things and people, His judgments—they proclaimed His purposes. For this they were inspired, not in any mechanical way, as if their individuality was lost and they became vocal instruments merely, but their whole being was filled and elevated while they were fulfilling this special purpose of declaring the word of the Lord. Their utterances were shaped by their several individualities, and they themselves were shaped by their times—they spoke in human language, "understanded of the people"—human passion, righteous indignation, natural and national sympathies, high, but not always pure and heavenly feeling, found voice in them—devotion to the God of Israel was a fire in their bones. And God used them to make Himself, His will, His approbation or His displeasure, known to His chosen people—"At sundry times, and in divers manners, God spake to the fathers by the prophets." How else should He speak? By psalm and sermon, in denunciation and warning, in tender entreaty, in pathetic reminder of what He was to them and had done for them, in inspiriting encouragement and promise, as Lawgiver, Judge and King, from the mysterious glories of the Temple, from the very circle of the heavens, in the Thunders of Sinai, and in the still, small voice, He spake to and through the prophets of those ancient times.

And the burden of it all was *righteousness*. A worthy theme for His inspiration of men. Even prophets could only partially take it in— they were pupil-teachers at best, these prophets of Israel. But they taught principles deeper than they understood—principles exhaustless in their application. They applied them only to present emergencies of national and personal life and character, but the Holy Ghost spake through them to all ages and to all sorts and conditions of men; and in their utterances we read for ourselves, between the lines, the unchanging mind and will of God, as applied to our circumstances and to ourselves.

In this view of the broad purpose and uses of the Bible, how comparatively insignificant are many of the questions now raised about it. Prove a text spurious, or a popular interpretation of it unsound or uncritical, and what does it matter in the large? Not one-thousandth part of the text of the Scriptures has ever been questioned by any criticism that has the slightest claim to be considered weighty or respectable. Probably some of you have been discomforted by the fear that these dreadful critics are trying to prove that only one-thousandth part of it is to be received. Your fears are groundless. In general, modern criticism is going on legitimate and reverent lines. There is comparatively little of it of that often flippant and mainly destructive sort, which has attained of late for two or three of our clergy, a melancholy notoriety because they are so conspicuously exceptional; who abuse their liberty, and try the forbearance of the Church, which does not easily bring itself to limit freedom of enquiry.

We hear much, for instance, of what is now called the "higher criticism," and with the notion many people have, that criticism means simply fault-finding, we are shocked at the idea that presumptuous men are "sitting in judgment on the Word of God." Criticism does not mean fault-finding; it means truth-finding. Most scriptural critics are reverent as well as scholarly men. They believe in God, and believe that God has spoken to men, and their aim is to find what God has really spoken. They study the language, they search out the history of the writings, they want to find out what is God's Word, and what it really means—most of them, at any rate. And as to the "higher criticism" of these later days, it does not mean a higher degree of fault-findingness. The term is used to describe a line of investigation differing from what is called textual criticism. That is confined to the question as to what is the true text of Scripture, and any one who knows anything of the history of the Sacred Book, and how it has gotten into its present shape, knows that such enquiries are not only legitimate, but necessary. For example: Is the story of the woman taken in adultery really a part of the Gospel written by St. John? Not, is the story true? Probably it *is* true—but for reasons, which I need not stop to give, the conclusion of scholars generally is that it is one of those "many other things which Jesus did, that are not written in this book," but which, because it was true, and because it was so good and characteristic of Him, some copyist added in the margin, and so some later copyist from the first copy inserted in the text. To determine questions like this is the province of textual criticism. But whether the book was written by St. John, or by some disciple of St. John; whether the whole prophecy of Isaiah was written by that prophet, or part of the book by some one else, as a continuation of the prophet's work; and when the second part was written, by whom, and where; and how can the interpreter best put himself in the place and amid the surroundings of the writer, and what these were—all this is in the province of the higher and larger range of enquiry which is so much occupying Biblical students now.* There is use for both sorts of scholarly criticism, and there is nothing to be afraid of, speaking broadly, in the interest of truth. On the contrary, the thing to be afraid of is *non-enquiry;* and that the idea that the Bible will not bear the literary and historical investigation given to other ancient writings should gain ground among irreligious, or even among religious men. I believe that a large part of the active antagonism to the Bible, in our day, and a still larger part of that quiet and satisfied indifference to it which passes under the name of agnosticism, is the natural reaction of an enquiring age against a blind conservatism on the part of its interpreters. What we may call the traditional view of Scripture—though, indeed, the tradition has no great venerableness, it only runs back about three centuries—has become impossible. That view, which is that every letter of the Bible is Divinely placed, and that every statement in it is to be literally interpreted, was never heard of before the sixteenth century, and will never be heard of after the nineteenth. Whose fault that is, or

---

* "It is the business of the critic to trace back the steps by which any ancient book has been transmitted to us, to find where it came from, and who wrote it, to examine the occasion of its composition, and search out every link that connects it with the history of the ancient world, and with the personal life of the author."—W. Robertson Smith, O. T. in Jewish Ch., p. 25.

whether it be a fault, or even a misfortune, is not now a useful question, but the fact remains that a great many people's ideas about the Bible are upset. But the Bible is not upset, any more than the earth has been upset by the geological questions and their answers, which have come up in the last 300 years. The earth is exactly what it was before the geologists began to enquire what it was, and it is just as safe a place to live in. So the Bible is just what it was for 1500 years of the life the Catholic Church of Christ lived on it, and before there was pressed on Christendom, by the apparent emergencies of the controversy with Rome, a theory of the Bible which scholars have found to be untenable, and which even Protestants have, of late, been taking much pains to disprove.

I want to have you take in the fact that the Episcopal Church has never held or taught any such theory. She holds what the early Church held, and has no utterances to take back or revise, and has endorsed no theory as to the exact nature and method of the inspiration of Holy Scripture. What she holds you will find in the sixth Article of Religion, which please to read without any modern and ultra-Protestant annotations:

"Holy Scripture containeth all things necessary to salvation; so that whatsoever is not read therein, nor may be proved thereby, is not to be required of any man, that it should be believed as an Article of the Faith or be thought requisite or necessary to salvation. In the name of the Holy Scripture we do understand those canonical Books of the Old and New Testament, of whose authority was never any doubt in the Church."

This is the rational and historical ground on which we stand, and may safely rest. The Church is the witness and keeper of Holy Writ, and Christendom is wiser than any Christian— knows more, and is a better interpreter. It does not undertake to tell how and in what measure the inspiration of the human writers of Holy Scripture makes their words Divine; but Divine in a very real and sufficient sense they are, as conveying to us the mind and will of God. Neither literal inspiration nor literal interpretation is sound, rational, or churchly; but the Bible is a book which cannot be accounted for on any other supposition than that somehow God put it into the world, that He "caused all Holy Scripture to be written for our learning."

It is worthy of its Author and its purpose. All the books of the Bible, written by so many men, through so many centuries, have one tone, one spirit, one purpose, teach one lesson—righteousness as towards men, reverence and obedience as towards God. This one note is the sufficient proof that the men who wrote them were inspired by *One Spirit*. Where else will you find *righteousness* taught under the sanction of accountability? And, rightly read, it conveys a worthy and worshipful conception of the Supreme

Being. Where, in other so-called sacred books, will you find even a manly God? But here is set forth One Whom we can worship with self-respect; Whose worship exalts, purifies, teaches and restrains; in Whose image we were made, and Whose communion, inspiration and teaching elevates each one who lives in it into that highest product of the intelligent creation—a *godly man.*

GOD'S PURPOSE IN THE LIFE OF JOSEPH.

S. JOHN'S, STAMFORD, JULY 14, 1878.

GOD'S PURPOSE IN THE LIFE OF JOSEPH.

"Ye thought evil against me; but God meant it unto good."—GENESIS l. 20.

The history of Joseph is the history of one on whom Divine mercy was so increased and multiplied, that, God being his Ruler and Guide, he so passed through things temporal that he finally lost not the things eternal. And as his life was in this respect, so may everybody else's be. For God's purpose in the life of Joseph was, (1) to bring out what was in him, (2) to use it for the good of others, (3) and in doing so to make the most of him, for this world and the world to come. And such a primary purpose there is on God's part for every human life, and the only thing that can hinder His carrying it out for us is our own perverseness, which drives Him back, so to speak, on His secondary and alternative plan, making Him do *the best He can* with us, in default of doing *the best He would*.

If we keep this in mind we shall not wonder that thirteen chapters of the Bible are occupied with this representative history. It is recorded simply because it is representative and not because it is peculiar. It may be, in substance, your history and mine, a history of providential opportunities and their improvements.

When we find the key to any human life we can interpret it. But usually the key is not found until toward the close of life, when we can infer the Divine purpose in it from what it has actually accomplished, or from what it has conspicuously failed to accomplish. We can best interpret the Divine purpose in the life of Joseph by starting with the results of it, and going backward over his career. We see then that circumstances did not make the man, but rather the man his circumstances. The conditions of his life were shaped, at its several crises, by his character.

The outcome of Joseph's life, so far as this world is concerned, is to be found in the character and history of the Hebrew nation, which he so largely shaped and influenced. Why "Israel abode in Egypt, and Jacob was a stranger in the land of Ham," is not difficult to see. At the period in the history of that people in which Joseph appears upon the scene, the family had grown into a tribe, and in the 400 years following it, the tribe developed into a nation. It was a period of growth in numbers, of consolidation, and of the formation of a national habit and tradition as a peaceful and pastoral people, whose normal condition, though they could fight, and fight well on occasion, was yet very different from that of the predatory tribes of Palestine. If the family of Jacob had remained in their own land they must have

GOD'S PURPOSE IN THE LIFE OF JOSEPH.

come to be like the Canaanitish nations, wanderers over the face of the country, unsettled, and incapable of the higher forms of civilization such as prevailed in Egypt. They would have had to hold their own against continual aggressions of their neighbors, or to become absorbed in some powerful existing tribe or nation which could protect them—their separate existence as a peculiar people would have been imperilled. But the fitness of things required that God's peculiar people should not be a band of robbers, but should be turned to legitimate pursuits. And a quiet pastoral tribe, in training for a high degree of political and spiritual examination, could only be developed into material for such a nation under the protection of another and powerful people with settled institutions. And yet, on the other hand, these institutions must be essentially alien to them. They must not assimilate with the Egyptians, they must live secure among them for a time, but distinct in race, in politics, and in religion. This result was signally attained. As shepherds, they were an abomination to the Egyptians. On both sides there was repulsion and not attraction, and they never became a part of the people among whom they dwelt. Theirs was a peculiar history, for a peculiar purpose. The favor of the Pharaohs was necessary to nourish them during their infancy as a nation, until the time came when the disfavor of the Pharaohs was necessary to wean them from their home in the house of bondage. While the influence and honored memory of Joseph lasted—Zaphnath-paaneah, the saviour of the age—they were protected but not absorbed, until "another king arose who knew not Joseph" and the necessary experience of oppression aroused them to the assertion of an independent national character and existence.

Here, then, we see the broad result, and in the result the broad purpose in Joseph's life, and having this key we can go backward and interpret his personal history, and see how that was shaped by his personal character.

In order to become the agent in so great a matter as the establishing of Israel in Egypt, Joseph must be a man who could control a kingdom, and not merely influence a king. His work was not only to make a Pharaoh willing to acquire new subjects, but also to make the Egyptians willing to receive into their territory an alien tribe for whom and whose pursuits they had an hereditary antipathy. This was a large demand on personal influence—he must be a large benefactor to the people, or the results of his influence with the king would be but temporary and partial. He must be, not a courtier, but a statesman, and a statesman of such personal character as to inspire an enthusiasm of popular affection and respect that would sustain him through a long life and administration, and would long attach to his memory as a national benefactor. He must be, and be known to be, a strong and good man, neither strong and bad, nor weak and good. And so we find in Joseph the two elements of power—the power of intellect and will, and the power of moral goodness resting on religious faith. A strong man, who believes in God, is always a power in the world. For, if the popular confidence in a man's ability gives him power, the popular confidence in his integrity and unselfishness consolidates and perpetuates it.

Look, therefore, at Joseph's public policy for evidence of his ability. His policy was *to strengthen the central government*, undoubtedly the best policy for the time. The famine gave him the opportunity. He made the people dependent on the crown; for when, notwithstanding the seven years' warning, the famine found them individually unprepared, it found government prepared with ample stores of provision, in return for which, under the astute management of the prime minister, the people parted with everything that gave them power. They parted with their money in the first year, with their cattle and horses in the second year, with their land in the third year, and, finally, with their liberties. "Buy us and our land for bread, and we and our land will be servants unto Pharaoh." Thus the monarchy became absolute. and that not by any usurpation, but by the free submission of the people—by a fair plebiscit;

and they felt that they had received a concession from the royal magnanimity, when Joseph restored to them the income from four-fifths of their surrendered property. He had turned one-fifth of the annual produce of the country into the royal exchequer, and thus secured a legitimate revenue which should amply sustain the state; and he had made the people sensible of their indebtedness to the wisdom and generosity of a paternal government for all their personal rights in life and property. There probably never was a despotism built, apparently, on so strong a foundation of justice as this of the Pharaohs, under the administration of Joseph, in which the rights were so clear on one side, and the duties so clear on the other, and in which the relations of government and people were so cemented by gratitude and affection. The effect of Joseph's policy was to make the people feel that they were in the power of the monarchy, and that, at least, under his administration they could trust it.

And it deserves notice, in further illustration of his statesmanship, that in attaching the people to the crown he accomplished the difficult task of avoiding the jealousy of a powerful class. He got the influence of the priesthood in favor of the new order of things by exempting their property from taxation. At the same time he strengthened the kingdom abroad and enriched it, by opening its markets to purchasers of grain from neighboring nations, and laid in this way the foundations of a commercial prosperity which lasted for many ages.

The effect of this wise, beneficent, far-seeing, and successful policy of the prime minister was to give him an influence almost unbounded with king and people, and to secure for him and all his belongings all that they could possibly ask from either. And when the house of Israel came to seek shelter and nourishment in the land, they came not uninvited or unwelcomed, but the warm and hearty interest of king, and court, and people, indicated the affection and enthusiasm which their powerful kinsman had inspired. "The fame thereof was heard in Pharaoh's house, saying, 'Joseph's brethren are come'; and it pleased Pharaoh well and his servants. And Pharaoh spake unto Joseph, saying, 'Thy father and thy brethren are come unto thee; the land of Egypt is before thee; in the best of the land make thy father and thy brethren to dwell.'" And so God's plan for Israel began to work.

We have reason therefore to be interested in the personality of the man through whose agency new institutions were impressed upon the most powerful nation of antiquity, and through whom, also, Israel received its opportunity of growth and development into material for the people and Church of God.

He grew into his high position as prime minister of Egypt and the saviour of the age, *simply by do-*

ing his duty in that state of life unto which it had pleased God to call him. This and nothing else is the open secret of his success. He was morally, as well as intellectually, equal to his opportunities. And God gave him opportunities. That is the story of his life. It was a life of great vicissitudes, but the one principle, of duty to God and his neighbor, ran through it all.

He was sold into slavery at seventeen years old. He became governor of all the land of Egypt at thirty. The thirteen years between these two ages are the period in which, as a general rule, the character of a man is settled, and the conditions of his life are determined.

Being such as he was, his misfortunes, even, were stepping-stones to success. It seemed to be a misfortune when in his simplicity he told his dreams, and aroused the envy of his brothers to the point of intended murder, and the slight accident, as it seemed, but real providence, occurred, of the Midianite merchantmen happening, just at that moment, to be passing just that way. His history would have been different but for any one of a thousand converging incidents that none but an overruling Providence, to whom nothing is small, could or would have shaped and guided. And so he was taken away from being spoiled by his father, and thrown out upon the world to make his way, but guided still. He became the slave of Potiphar, and so faithfully did his duty that he made him overseer in his house, and left all that he had in Joseph's hand. He was on the high-road to a small prosperity when a great adversity appeared to overtake him. The malice of an impure woman ruined his prospects, as it seemed, and he was cast into prison, with tarnished reputation, but with an untarnished character still, and he gravitated by the irrepressible force of character into an humble but useful position of trust again. Another opportunity was afforded him. By sympathy and kindness, as well as by his skill in interpretation, he won the confidence and gratitude of one of the king's servants. Not much gratitude, indeed, but when the king was in need of similar service the chief butler remembered what the young Hebrew had done for him, and made his own account, no doubt, in introducing him to Pharaoh. If his interpretation of the king's dreams was supernatural, his wise and statesmanlike counsel upon them was natural, as we would say with equal truth or untruth as the case may be, for Pharaoh had a juster view of inspiration when he attributed it all to God, and said, "Can we find such a one as this is—a man in whom the spirit of God is ? Forasmuch as God hath showed thee all this, there is none so discreet and wise as thou art: thou shalt be over my house, and according unto thy word shall all my people be ruled. See, I have set thee over all the land of Egypt."

So God made use of Joseph for the benefit of others. In doing so He brought out what was in him. He brought out his *self-control* for one thing. He who was to control a king and his kingdom had learned to control himself—to control his resentments and his affections alike. His treatment of his brothers shows that he was not to be run away with by either.

The combination of strength and tenderness in his character comes out in his punishment of his brethren for their good, and not for his satisfaction; and in his cordial forgiveness of them at the proper time, and in the gentlemanly lightening for them of their burden of remorse, so soon as they were indisposed to lighten it for themselves. "It was not you that sent me hither, but God."

In several ways the resoluteness of the man comes out—settling his policy and resolutely pursuing it; his fortitude under trials; his resistance to temptation—if he had yielded to impurity we may be sure he never would have become the man he was; his industry—giving his personal supervision to the distribution of the corn. "He it was that sold to all the people of the land."

In one word, it was faithfulness to duty that made him what he grew to be—faithfulness in all details of duty to his neighbor, whether the neighbor were father, or brother, or sovereign—Israelite or Egyptian.

Nor did he fail in his duty toward God. He recognized the ruling hand of Divine providence in each event of life. He believed in God, and feared, and loved Him; he put his whole trust in Him; he attributed to Him all the good he did, and gave God the glory in his successes. "God hath made me a father to Pharaoh, and ruler throughout all the land of Egypt." And, notwithstanding his great inducements to a contrary worldliness, he cherished what we may call his churchmanship; his heart was with the people of God, and he cast in his lot with them, was not ashamed to call them brethren before everybody, and in his last injunctions showed that he preferred a modest grave in the Holy Land to a royal tomb in an Egyptian pyramid.

Bringing out thus what was in Joseph, and using it for the benefit of others, God did him the highest honor that can be done for any human being. And in doing it, He rewarded him by making him the more of a man, and this is always the great reward of faithfulness. Joseph never at any time seems to have concerned himself about getting on, but he got on, notwithstanding, and that by a law of moral gravitation. He was a great man, and when God gave him the opportunity of great position and great usefulness, he greatly filled them. This was his reward here. So, with God for his ruler and guide, Joseph passed "through things temporal."

And we may safely say that he did not lose

"the things eternal." When a man thus grows great in this world, he does not cease to be great when he leaves it. Such as he goes out of this life, such he goes into the next. Not as to the accidents of his position; "he shall carry nothing away with him when he dieth, neither shall his pomp follow him." But as to the essentials of his character, he, himself, with all that God and he have made him, is the same man on the other side the grave that he is on this. What Joseph's position is in the other world, we do not know; but of this we may be sure, that it is one of influence commensurate with his attainments in power, and character, and influence in this—a ruler over ten cities. For God's plan in the life of Joseph extended over both worlds. Does it startle any one to hear me speak of any man's influence in the other world ? And why not ? That is no state of passionless repose, and if there is activity there, there is the eternal distinction between the strongly good and the weakly good; the leaders of men are there, and their followers, leading and following still.

The lesson of Joseph's history is this: That God is the Protector of all that trust in Him; that He has a purpose in the life of every man; that to effect this purpose He requires our acceptance of it, and our co-operation; that we should take Him for our Ruler and Guide; that we can only be sure that God is guiding us, and we are submitting to His guidance, when we are doing our duty in that state of life, whatever it may be, into which God has already called us. One step at a time, taken with good conscience, and we "so pass through things temporal that we finally lose not the things eternal."

THE ATONEMENT.

GOOD FRIDAY, S. JOHN'S, STAMFORD, APRIL 15, 1881.

THE ATONEMENT.

THE EXPLANATION WHICH THE SCRIPTURE GIVES OF THE REASON OF CHRIST'S DEATH.

"It is not possible that the blood of bulls and of goats should take away sins. Wherefore, when HE *cometh into the world He saith, Sacrifice and offering Thou wouldest not, but a body hast Thou prepared Me. In burnt offerings and sacrifices for sin Thou hast had no pleasure. Then said I, Lo, I come (in the volume of the book it is written of me) to do Thy will, O God. . . . By the which will we are sanctified through the offering of the body of Jesus Christ once for all."*—HEBREWS x. 4, 5, 6, 7, 10.

"By His own blood He entered in once into the holy place, having obtained eternal redemption for us."—HEB. ix. 12.

The Apostle, writing of the Atonement, represents Jesus as saying, "A body hast Thou prepared Me," "I come to do Thy will, O God."

He said this either as an individual or as a representative.

If He made this submission to the will of God as an individual, however exalted, and however exceptionally constituted by union of the Divine and human natures in Himself, then He either submitted *instead* of us, in which case we have not submitted, and the benefit of His submission

---

NOTE.—For the argument of this sermon at length, see Norris's Rudiments of Theology, "Soteriology of the Bible."

can only pass to us by imputation, or else He submitted in order to be an *example* to us, and we can only receive benefit from what He did by following His example.

This last is the explanation given of Christ's work by those who explain away the Atonement, and say that each man must be, after all, his own saviour, by living such a life of obedience to God, as Christ, his great exemplar, lived. *This is not Christianity.* It is true that we ought to follow the example of Christ, but it is also true that we do not follow it—cannot so follow it as to merit by doing so the favor of God. We cannot atone personally for our personal sins.

Nor is it true that the obedience of Christ is imputed to us, counted as *our* obedience, so that we take His place in the approbation and favor of God, and He takes our place in God's disapprobation and disfavor—we enjoying the rewards of His righteousness and He suffering the punishment of our sins. That is a statement of the doctrine of the Atonement which is often made, but it cannot be made to appear to the conscience otherwise than utterly unreal and unjust. And, moreover, let it be remembered in opposition to a meaning which has been read into many passages of Scripture, but has not been derived from Scripture, that it is nowhere said that Christ endured the punishment, paid the penalty of sin *instead of us.* For what is the

THE ATONEMENT.

penalty of sin? "The wages of sin is death." If by this is meant physical death, Christ indeed suffered it, but we do not escape it. If eternal death is meant, we, indeed, may escape it, but Christ does not suffer it. If spiritual death is meant—alienation of the soul from God—then, indeed, we may be delivered from that, but it were blasphemy to represent Christ as suffering it, as alienated from God, spiritually dead. In no sense is Christ substituted for us in enduring the penalty of sin. He bore our sin, but not our punishment. The Israelite never conceived of the innocent victim which he offered, as bearing his punishment. He did conceive of it as typically bearing away his sin. And so we conceive of our Redeemer, as bearing away our sin, but not as suffering the penalty.

But if we understand Christ as submitting Himself to God as our Representative, if, taking *the body*, the perfect human nature which was prepared for Him, becoming not *a* man, but *The Man*, the Captain of our salvation, our Champion, our Sponsor, if human nature was gathered up into Him, then we understand that it was no mere personal act of submission that He made, but that in Him mankind has made its submission *to God*—has made an absolute surrender of everything, even to life itself, in the Sacrifice of the Cross. For this absolute and entire submission and surrender is the essential thing in any true relation of man to God. Human nature

THE ATONEMENT.

in Him answered to the charge, and pleaded guilty, and laid down its forfeited life—laid it down, that it might take it again.

The race of man, considered as a whole, and acting through the Divine Man, has submitted itself to the will of God; it remains for each individual of the race to accept and ratify that submission for his personal self. Man is redeemed; it remains for men to appropriate that redemption to the saving of their souls, or reject it to their loss and ruin. To appropriate redemption, by faith, through the Sacraments generally necessary to salvation. In all the occurrences of the Week of the Passion, and the Day of the Crucifixion, we must think of Jesus, not as separated from us by that individuality by which we are separated from and independent of each other, but as one with us, so that human nature found voice to groan in Gethsemane under the burden of conscious sin, and on Calvary it felt the darkness sin makes between the spiritual eye of man and the face of God. He suffered not *instead* of Man, but man suffered in Him; Man in Him atoned for man's sin; *the Divine Man was crucified,* and all mankind died in Him to sin, that mankind in Him might live unto God.

Keeping this inseparable relation of Christ to us always in our thought, underlying all we further say, let us go on to say, most distinctly and definitely, that *the Scripture representation*

THE ATONEMENT.

of Christ's redemptive work makes it to consist not in His life, but in His death. In the fulfilment of the will of God "we are sanctified, *through the offering of the body of Jesus Christ once for all.*"

The aspect under which Christ's work for our redemption is presented, from the beginning of Scripture to the end of it, is the aspect of *sacrifice*. And that, not the sacrifice of will merely, not sacrifice merely in doing or suffering, but the sacrifice of life. "Without shedding of blood is no remission," is the keynote of the written word of God. The life of man was forfeited by sin, and religion consisted first of all in the acknowledgment of this. It was expressed, until, in the fulness of time, the Lamb of God was slain, in the animal sacrifices that prefigured the One Sacrifice. The offering of Abel was acceptable, and the offering of Cain was not, because the one acknowledged that his life was forfeited by sin, and he had no righteousness in himself, while the other undertook to assert his own sufficiency, and to make God his debtor by a gift of what he had himself produced. Abraham's act of faith expressed the surrender of forfeited life, and the revelation was made to him of a Redeemer. When God redeemed the first-born of Israel from death, the blood upon the door-posts was the sign, and he claimed the redeemed first-born as His, making the Passover lamb the perpetual sign of the covenant of redemption. And all through the provisions Divinely ordained for the worship of the chosen people, ran the idea that human life was forfeited by human sin, and redeemed by the sacrifice of life, the blood of bulls and goats, which of themselves could never take away sin, but could only foreshadow the taking away of sin by the sacrifice of man himself in the death of the Representative Man.

This afternoon we shall read for the first lesson the wonderful depiction by Isaiah of the suffering Saviour, in the fifty-third chapter—the text from which the Evangelist Philip began his instructions to the Ethiopian eunuch, and "preached unto him Jesus." In that description of the redemptive work of Christ there is no mention even of His *teaching,* no mention of His *example,* no mention of His *inaugurating a society or kingdom for the salvation of men.* The burden of the prophecy is suffering and death. He is "a man of sorrows, and acquainted with grief," "He hath borne our griefs and carried our sorrows," "He was wounded for our trangressions, He was bruised for our iniquities, the chastisement of our peace was upon Him, and with His stripes we are healed"; and "the Lord hath laid on Him the iniquity of us all," "He was cut off out of the land of the living," "He made His grave with the wicked, and with the rich in His death," His soul is made "an offering for sin." In this, the principal Messianic prophecy of the Old Testament Scriptures, it is the death —the suffering and death of the Redeemer— that is dwelt upon, and not His teaching and His life.

And when we turn to the New Testament, whither we must turn if we would find Christ's own account, and His immediate disciples' account of the nature of His work for man, we are struck at once with the fact that the narrative in the Gospel leads up to and evidently culminates in the Passion and Crucifixion. Thirty-three years of His life occupy one-half of the Gospels, and one week occupies the other half. And not only that, but all through the first half there is a looking forward, a continually recurring reference to the end. The end was always full in the Redeemer's view. "I have a baptism to be baptized with, and how am I straitened until it be accomplished." To Nicodemus He said, "As Moses lifted up the serpent in the wilderness, even so must the Son of Man be lifted up"— "this said He, signifying what death He should die." "The bread that I will give is My Flesh, which I will give for the life of the world." He is the Good Shepherd, and "the Good Shepherd giveth His life for the sheep." "I lay down my life, that I might take it again." "The Son of Man came . . . to give His life a ransom for many." "I, if I be lifted up, will draw all men unto Me." "The hour is come that the Son of Man should be glorified. Verily, verily,

THE ATONEMENT.

I say unto you, except a corn of wheat fall into the ground and die, it abideth alone: but if it die, it bringeth forth much fruit." All the harvest is contained in the seed-corn. And how often He had to reiterate to His disciples, who, after all, could not take it in, "that the Son of Man must suffer many things, . . . and be killed, and after three days rise again." That Christ was our Teacher and our Example it is not necessary to prove, but how little does He Himself dwell upon these characters of Himself in comparison with the character of a suffering Saviour, dying for men, *The Sacrifice.*

After bringing before you Christ's own teaching about Himself and the nature of His redemptive work for man, it seems to me unnecessary to go through the sermons and letters of the Apostles as we find them in the remainder of the New Testament. They teach no other doctrine than Himself taught. He is to them always the Lamb of God, taking away the sin of the world. The text may stand for them all, and the teaching of that is, that Christ took our nature upon Him and stood for mankind—that He was the Real Sacrifice, which others had only typified—that we are reconciled to God in virtue of His atoning death.

But it is worth while to dwell for another moment on the fact that the great act of worship which He instituted—the Lord's Supper—is a perpetual memorial of His Sacrifice. He will

THE ATONEMENT.

not suffer us to forget that He died for us. The Body was broken and the Blood was shed—this is the one thing to be remembered. The central fact of the Christian religion is the Sacrifice of the death of Christ.

But let us remember—for we must be again and again recalled to this thought—that it is not as One outside of us, as a substitute for us, that He sacrificed Himself, but *as One in whom we were and are,* as our *Sponsor,* as our *federal Head.* His submission to the Father is not *imputed* to us; it is *our* submission, made by the only One except Adam, who had the capacity and the right to speak and act for the race of man.

I think this helps us dimly to see, not *a* reason, not *the* reason, but reason for the Sacrifice of the death of Christ. It is a mystery, and probably must ever remain a mystery, why "the wages of sin is death," why life is forfeited by it. Why sin entered the world we never can understand; *but it did enter.* And why death entered the world by sin we cannot understand; *but it did enter the world by sin.* And certain it is that every disturbance of the moral order must have *some* ill consequence. These are facts which we cannot ignore—we do not believe them; *we know them.* And while it is of course not necessary that we should see all that is in the mind of God as the reason for the Atonement of Jesus Christ in order that we should believe in it, yet some perception, some instinct of it, *will help our faith*. This is the chief value of any effort to relieve our minds of needless confusions, perplexities, difficulties, in connection with fundamental doctrines of religion—to help our faith. And the human heart wants to believe in an Atonement. In our consciousness of guilt and ill-desert we crave a Divine Redeemer, a sufficient Sacrifice. Explain as we may how it got there, there is, deep down in the soul of man, a belief in sacrifice. And yet we want at the same time to believe in the love and in the truth of God; we *must* believe them. And we must free our conceptions of God from all suspicion of hardness, of vengefulness, of injustice, of unreal dealing with the facts of human sin and weakness; from all notions of the Son appeasing a Father's wrath, of a transaction between the justice and the mercy of Deity, of vicarious endurance of penalty, of compensation for sin. The full meaning of this day's tremendous incidents we may not be able to comprehend on this side the grave; but we know that there are some things which they cannot mean. God is love. Christ has redeemed us from sin. We have died, in Him, to sin, have no business with it, no relation to it; it is outside of our redeemed and regenerated selves. And in proportion as we realize by faith this fact of our death in Him unto sin, we shall also realize our new birth in Him unto righteousness. Righteousness will be the law of our life, working itself out progressively in our life, and we as individual men will become what man has been made, "dead indeed unto sin, but alive unto God, through Jesus Christ our Lord."

THE INTERCESSION OF CHRIST.

SECOND MORNING LESSON. SUNDAY AFTER ASCENSION, S. JOHN'S, STAMFORD, MAY 6, 1894.

THE INTERCESSION OF CHRIST.

"And now I am no more in the world, but these are in the world, and I come to Thee. Holy Father, keep through Thine own Name those whom Thou hast given me." "I pray not that Thou shouldest take them out of the world, but that Thou shouldest keep them from the evil."—S. JOHN xvii. 11, 15.

This prayer of Christ for His disciples, uttered in the expectation of His Ascension, was intended to give them and us the comfort of the thought that He who is gone into heaven, and sitteth at the right hand of God, "ever liveth to make intercession for us." He has assumed His mediatorial kingdom, He has taken His place as the Representative of our humanity at the court of heaven. He gathers up into Himself all our relations with Deity, and throws over all our sinfulness and infirmity the covering of His own righteousness and strength. As our great High Priest within the veil, He mingles with the breath of all our supplications the incense of His own prevailing intercession, and when we ask anything in His Name, He says, "Father, I will."

"And now," He says, "I am no more in the world, but these are in the world." We have here a suggestion of His infinite tenderness for those whom He was about to leave; of the close, personal relation into which His heart had entered with those who had been so long with Him. It was not a merely official relation. He did not regard them simply as instruments which He could use for His own purposes. His Divinity did not overshadow the gentler qualities of our human nature, and the fact that He had a charity which embraced the world in its purpose, did not withdraw from the inner circles in which His human life was passed the genial grace of personal sympathy. In His exaltation He remembers their bereavement—their weakness which He had strengthened, their ignorance which He had enlightened—and anticipates the desolateness which will come over them when He has departed, Who had been their dependence and their joy. His yearning heart gives utterance then to a burst of prayer, "Holy Father, keep them! Keep, through Thine own Name, those whom Thou hast given Me!"

Dwelling first of all on His immediate followers, His prayer expands to take in the work, and He follows them with His benediction through all the Christian centuries. "Neither pray I for these alone, but for them also which shall believe on Me through their word."

Consider, therefore, this prayer of Christ for His disciples then and now, as it indicates the relation of the Christian to the evil which is in the world. His separation from it is not to be local. "I pray not that Thou shouldest take them out of the world." It is to be a moral separation—"but that Thou shouldest keep them from the evil."

Here is the principle recognized that the Christian has relations to the world which he cannot ignore. This is the view of Christ; but it is not the view which we should be apt to take of it. We are quite as likely to fall in with the Pharisaic idea of a local separation from evil as to recognize the position of the Christian to be what our Lord elsewhere described it, as "the salt of the earth." The Pharisee divided off mankind, as many others have done, into saints and sinners; Pharisees and publicans must stand far off from one another, and Jews have no dealings with Samaritans. But Christ recognized a brotherhood which lay deeper than theological differences, and which was not destroyed by the widest divergency of moral character. And so He Who in His earthly walk was "holy, harmless, undefiled, and separate from sinners," yet never shunned their companionship. He was a guest in their houses, He ate and drank with them, He received them, and so they received Him. The scorn of those who assumed to be the exponents of morality and religion had hardened these sinners in their sins; but here was One Whose life was holy, yet He shunned them not. There was something good in them. At least there was the wish to be better than they were; and so He found the joints of their armor with His winged words of kindness, and subdued them with His love. What wonder that such a One, adopting a course so unprecedented and uttering words so new, should have had a large following among the poor and outcast, and that "this people which knoweth not the law" should have responded to the Gospel!

The example of the Master was followed by the disciples. They did not gather themselves into a close corporation for the enjoyment and preservation of truth and goodness. They were missionaries. "Go ye into all the world," He said, and they went. How signally they illustrated this missionary spirit of Christianity! How they plunged into the midst of heathenism, fearless of the evil there was in it, and trustful of the good with which they were charged for the world's benefit! How they shrank not from the darkness of ignorance, bearing the light of Christian truth! How they made religion a practical, and not a speculative thing, applying it to the common, every-day spiritual needs of the many, in opposition to the notions of the Jews, who thought it the property of a favored few, and those few a sect chosen out of a nation, which nation was chosen out from the world! They had drunk deeply of the catholic spirit of their Master, and had appreciated this prayer of His for them: "I pray not that Thou shouldest take them out of the world."

And this, too, is His prayer for us, and this the

lesson for us, of His own and His disciples' lives. To be *in* the world, yet not *of* the world, and to be drawn closer to Him in our inner life as we the more fully "do our duty in that state of life unto which it has pleased God to call us."

This prayer of Christ, that God would not take His followers out of the world, is offered for the world's sake, and for their own. For the world's sake—for, inadequate as it is, the influence of Christian people in the world is the best influence the world knows. It is an utter assumption on the part of some, to stand in the midst of a society leavened by the influence of Christianity, and deny it the credit of its work, while freely noting the deficiencies of its followers. Poor sponsors are they for the virtues of the nineteenth century who stand and scoff at the mother that bore them all. We shall best appreciate personal Christian influence in the world when we undertake to form a conception of the state of the world without it. What charities would cease if that law should be repealed. "This commandment have we received from Him, that he who loveth God should love his brother also"; and if the inspiration of that motive were withdrawn, "Beloved, if God so loved us, we ought also to love one another"; and that measure of the measureless love of God, "God so loved the world that He gave His Only-begotten Son!" What iniquities would burst their bounds if the restraint should be relaxed in which these words hold the passions of men, "We must all appear before the judgment-seat of Christ." For, we are to remember, that not the Bible holds the practical, working force of Christianity so much as does the Church; it is not a Book which acts on the world directly, but men—thinking, acting, living men, moved by a living Spirit of God, meeting the evil of the world wherever it appears, and in whatever form, and, making as it were, an atmosphere congenial to all good. And so Christian men and women are not taken out of the world so soon as they are fit for a better, but left in it to sweeten and enlighten it. Deriving light themselves from the one true Light of the world, they are to distribute it from many centres. The Scripture says of Christians that they shine "as lights in the world," not dispelling the darkness, indeed, but doing something towards it, though not so much as they might do if the lights were brighter and there were more of them. It would be sad, indeed, if men and women could ever become, as we say, "too good for this world." We may be sure that *that* is not the reason good men die.

But there is another way of getting out of the world besides getting out through "the grave and gate of death." It is by secluding one's self from its temptations to evil, and therefore from its opportunities for good. I do not say this was in the thought of Jesus when He spoke the words of the text, for God does not take men out of the world in this way, and therefore there was no need to pray Him not to do so. And it is not usually religion, but indolence, that leads men so to take themselves out of the world of duty. Indolence, or some other subtle form of self-indulgence, it is, that leads men to keep out of politics because they are unsavory; and out of moral reform movements because they are troublesome, and often hopeless; and out of charitable work because "there is no end of it," as they sometimes say. How any Christian man can satisfy his conscience, with these words of Christ before him, embodying a principle, a precept for His disciples in a prayer to His Father, it is difficult to see. If they are not to be taken out of the world, then they are to be left in the world, and for a purpose; and the prayer that they may be kept from the evil, indicates that they are to face the evil, and not shun it. The purpose of the salt is to be effected, not in the salt-cellar, but on the meat; the place for the candle is not under the bushel, but on the candlestick, where it "giveth light unto all that are in the house." The religion is weak, unmanly, and therefore ungodly, that shrinks from encountering evil, and dealing with it. Especially with this prayer of Christ behind it, for Divine strength to be given to keep His followers from succumbing to the evil. The soul that is saved, if any is, by this sort of selfish and timorous policy, we may almost say is not worth saving.

And yet is not this, in some sort, the underlying thought of many of us who are afraid of our surroundings, and build spiritual air-castles, in which we would like to dwell apart, with all our temptations at safe distance, and everything about us favorable to a quiet and easy religious life? It is the old monkish idea that has such a charm for some temperaments, of shutting themselves out from the world, loosening their connection with its daily duties, and common cares, and secular interests, and social pleasures, as a step towards higher attainment in the Christian life. Indeed, I think that very many of us are liable to this error, when, weary and heartsick with the struggles and failures of our lives, as at present passed, we long for the wings of a dove, that we may flee away and be at rest. The manifold trials and vexatious cares which come to us in the circumstances in which God has placed us, seem to us like the clinging lime upon the wing of the snared bird, to hinder the flights of which we conceive our souls are capable. We take refuge from our self-accusings for commonplace duties left undone, and temptations only half resisted, in a sort of romantic dream of what we will do and be when our circumstances change, and we can have everything just right about us.

But the prayer of Christ is against us in this,

for these very circumstances in which we find ourselves are our world, and He asks that we may not be taken out of it. These hindering outward cares, these chilling influences of association, these business, or political, or social relations which we sustain—these are our world, which we cannot leave; this is the field on which we are to achieve our spiritual victories, if any. And the wish to get out of our own proper world of duty, and care, and interest, and pleasure, too, into some imagined world of circumstances, in which it would be easier for us to realize our own conceptions of the Christian life, is ignoble and faithless. It is a wish to be able to offer unto the Lord of that which doth cost us nothing. It is a failure of trust in God.

For in all this we lose sight of the main object of our probation here, and of an important means of attaining it. The object of our earthly life, so far as we ourselves are concerned, is the formation of a robust Christian character, and temptation is a means of attaining it. To form character, rather than to observe rules—to be, rather than to do. For character is enduring, eternal; our conduct is chiefly important as it makes us what we are, and indicates it.

And as we sometimes err in an estimate of the object to be attained, so we err sometimes in our judgment of individual failures in attaining it. We may call that effort a failure which does not achieve the special object intended in it, while in reference to the general end designed in the trial—the strengthening and developing of character—God may judge it, more broadly and truly, to be a success. There are many men, it has been suggested, "who might have been great in wickedness, but who, striving toward good, seem to show but little progress. There are many lives which, looked upon from without, are sad lives—so much endeavor, so little achievement (as the world judges); so much labor and pain, so little result. But who shall say that these lives are, in truth, one-half so sad as many lives of far more evident success?" The rolling of the stone up-hill in the ancient story seemed to be a vain and fruitless effort, but it developed the sinews of a giant; and a life of effort persevered in to the end, in spite of frequent failure, is not, in itself and on the whole, a failure.

To recognize in this way the office of temptation in our lives will help us to be satisfied with our conditions, and do the best we can under them, and not wish vainly for other conditions into which serious temptation shall not enter. This is our ideal of a life; we never introduce the element of temptation into our plans. But God does. We would hedge ourselves about with favoring circumstances. But God would put us out into the midst of difficulties. And in the eternity for which we are preparing, we shall see that God's plan of life is best.

THE INTERCESSION OF CHRIST.

But this, let us remember for our encouragement, is only half our Saviour's prayer, and we can only say *Amen* when He adds to this, "but that Thou shouldest keep them from the evil." As well give up the contest now, as carry it on in our own unaided strength. The evil of the world is worldliness, and we can be in the world without being worldly. *In* it in the fullest sense—alive to all its interests, quick to discern where our influence can be brought to bear upon it for good. "A man of the world," in the highest sense of that expression, only a Christian man can be, for he has power within him. Yet not *of* the world, inasmuch as the inspiration and moral power of our lives are from above.

And we may have confidence that so we shall be kept if we truly desire to be. For this part of the prayer of Christ is as efficacious as the other, and none of it is vain. This intercession of the Saviour for the Father's protection of those whom He had given Him is no unpractical expression of a vague and general good-will. We are all living and fighting under this shield. A life of duty and safety here, and reward hereafter, is in our power. In all our consciousness of infirmity, this prayer of Christ may comfort and encourage. The moral dangers and difficulties of life will diminish or disappear before the power and inspiration of faith, and we need not tremble if we will only trust. It sounds like the response of the Eternal Father to this intercession of Christ for those appointed to a life of trial, "As thy days, so shall thy strength be."

THE UNSOLVED PROBLEMS OF LIFE DISPOSED OF BY THE INCARNATION—GOD'S GIFT OF HIS SON.

EPISTLE, FIRST SUNDAY AFTER TRINITY, S. JOHN'S, STAMFORD,
JUNE 12, 1887.

THE UNSOLVED PROBLEMS OF LIFE DISPOSED OF BY THE INCARNATION —GOD'S GIFT OF HIS SON.

"God is Love. In this was manifested the love of God toward us, because that God sent His Only-begotten Son into the world, that the world through Him might have life."— I. JOHN iv. 8, 9.

The story of the Fall, which was read this morning in the Lesson from Genesis, seems at first sight almost to record the failure of creation. The world is not, apparently, what God intended it to be. He made man innocent and happy, but he fell into sin and into sorrow. The six days' work seems vain.

Nay, but wait till the end of the seventh day before you say so. Those were the days of physical forces, material creations and evolutions. This seventh period, in which we are now living, is the day of moral and spiritual forces, of moral and spiritual re-creation and evolution. What if it shall last as long as any of the former periods. At the end of all God will surely look upon His moral and spiritual creation, and see that it was good.

For, as in the preceding epochs of creation, force was struggling with intractable matter, so in this present epoch spiritual force from God is struggling with the intractable spiritual substance of human nature, and slowly but surely moulding human wills. The spiritual creation is still in process, growing towards completion, and when it is completed the eighth day will begin, with a moral world equipped for some further and higher development. For why should we think the Creator's work is to stop right here? God is *essentially* a Creator. He cannot stop; He is not exhausted of designs, or of power to carry them out. Why should we imagine it? Is what we know the boundary of knowledge? Is what we are the limit of Divine possibilities? We are immortal. What can we do in eternity but grow?

The force which God has put into this world —this human world of ours—to make it grow, and to evolve the perfected humanity which is His ideal, is a spiritual force, a Divine Life—the Life of His Incarnate Son, the Life of His sanctifying and regenerating Spirit. "The Spirit of God moved upon the face of the waters"; and still His Spirit broods over the deep of human nature, to bring a moral cosmos out of a moral chaos. Look broadly over the meaning of the world, and you will see that it is not a failure. For "God so loved the world that He sent His Only-begotten Son, that the world through Him might be saved." It is part of the process that we are here this morning. O, if we can only take it in! If we can only realize that in this,

His labors of the seventh day, we are co-workers with God! For in this He is not working with His mechanical and chemical forces upon matter, but with moral forces upon mind. His purpose now, in this seventh day's creative work, is *to make good men*. And good men are not negations of evil—innocent, simply, as our first parents were innocent, because they had not the knowledge of good and evil. The knowledge of good implies the knowledge of evil, and the choice of good implies the choice between the two. The question of moral goodness is the question of choice—of the choice of free and self-determining wills. There must be forbidden fruit. There must be a tempter. But there must also be Divine help. It is the Divine seed of the woman —the Incarnate God in human nature—that shall bruise the serpent's head, shall mortally wound the evil one, and the evil in every one.

And so the world and man are not a failure, but only, as yet, an incomplete success. They are not a failure, though once they might have seemed to be; and they will not be a failure, for God has set His infinite heart upon them, and is exerting upon them His infinite power. But that power is exerted under conditions inherent in the nature of the work to be done, and according to the laws which govern the case. And these conditions and laws have relation to the fact of human freedom. How every valuable result *for* man has to be wrought out *with* man—with his acceptance of the purpose and plan, his use of the means, his co-operation. And how much patience it calls for! And how much seeming failure of good is only success delayed! And so God has infinite patience under the processes—and why should He not? He has eternity before Him. How many myriads of years are included in each of the six days of creation which have passed, spent in making the material world as it is, and preparing it for the still grander and higher work now being wrought out upon it in the making of good men—men who *choose* goodness, and therefore *are* good. But what God's heart is set upon will surely come to pass, and this is what His heart is set upon, and no pains and no sacrifice has He spared—"God so loved the world that He gave His Only-begotten Son." And this is that which redeems the world from failure. The world that God so loved is not, and cannot be a failure. We cannot be pessimistic in view of this evidence of the love of God.

I. And yet, there are some very strange things about this world that God so loved. I shall only voice the unuttered but real perplexities of many minds if I recall some of the unsolved and insoluble problems which meet us at every turn in life. I do it in order to bring them face to face with this great announcement of the love of God. in the hope of helping some of you—not to solve, but to dispose of them, in the midst of things you know but cannot understand; to be still, and *know that God is God*, and, better still, to know that *God is Love*.

1. I will say nothing now about that greatest problem, *the origin of evil;* perhaps enough has been said to suggest the key to that mystery. Its possibility is a necessity to human freedom—its active origin is human, not Divine.

But what a problem is that which we meet with every day, in the fact of *irremediable evil done*—evil done which cannot be remedied, at any rate, by him who does it. For many of the wrongs men do to each other they can make restitution. But there are some wrongs that, so far as we can see, can never be righted. The blot left upon the soul of a child by your foul or profane word, uttered in a moment, and forgotten by you, but by him never—the stain remains. The doubt left by a strong mind, deliberately setting itself to undermine the faith of a weak one—the strong man may become a believer, but the seeds of infidelity he has sown along his way have sprouted and grown taller than he. The slanders upon reputations, which in very thoughtlessness you may have scattered —as well might you undertake to go back and gather up the thistledown you have blown as you crossed your neighbor's field, as to go back and recall your wanton slanders. These are illustrations of irremediable evil done. You repent, but the evil remains. It has become a factor in God's world. Oh, why am I not permitted to annihilate the evil I have created! But no, I cannot. Perplexity most awful! The perplexity of God's doing evil would not be greater than the perplexity of His permitting me to do evil which He does not permit me to undo.

2. Again, *useless sorrow and suffering.* Useless, because of much sorrow and suffering we can see the uses, and there is no perplexity about that. It works good often. It chastens, refines, purifies. It tries and strengthens faith. It enlarges charity. It develops the capacity for sympathizing. It is a hard discipline, but it *is* discipline, and discipline is good. But will any of you tell me the uses to be found in the suffering of animals? Has any father, or any mother yet discovered the uses in the suffering of children—young children, who wail, and wail, and cannot tell what hurts them, much less why? There is nothing in God's universe so hard, so inexplicable. We could see them die, and Christian faith would say, "Of such is the Kingdom of heaven," "because the child's soul pleased the Lord, therefore He hasted to take him away from among the wicked, lest that wickedness should darken his understanding, and deceit beguile his soul." But of the suffering which ends in death, or which does not end in death, we have no sufficient explanation.

3. And even *of the death of children*, though faith may have an explanation, nature has none. And, more generally, the useless waste of nature, the perishing buds and blossoms of all forms of life, what mysterious prodigality ! What large potentialities come to nothing ! Born, to accomplish nothing, only to feed the insatiable grave. And then, what wrenches of the heart that might have been spared, that ought to have been spared ! When Herod slaughtered the Innocents, what good did it do Herod ? What good the soldiers ? What good the mothers ? What good the world ? And we set apart a day with a service in the Prayer Book, to bring before our dazed eyes a ghastly iniquity, a useless waste of blood and feeling, a hard and cruel perplexity to human hearts, that almost challenge God to give an account of why He allows such things to be.

4. And then, again, another great perplexity —*the fact that so many people have no helps to goodness, only to badness.* Go, you who have books of devotion with red edges, and a hassock to kneel upon at a beautiful *prie-Dieu*, go into the stage-house yard, and enquire in one of the dwellings there, where is the closet into which the mother can go to say her prayers. See what the surroundings are out of which virtue and piety are expected to come. Or ask the drunkard, often, why he does not stay at home in the company of his wife and children—such a wife,

and such children !—instead of making a beast of himself at the tavern. Or ask the Italian boy in New York why he is not honest ; or the girl in the tenement house room where lodgers are taken in with the family, why she is not modest. Ask the ignorant why they know no better ; or the tainted why they are not clean. God only knows what might have been for all of these, and many more—if God is good, we ask why was it not?

5. *The prosperity of the wicked and the adversity of the righteous*, too, is a problem no nearer solution by unassisted nature than it was in David's time. There was John in the dungeon of the castle of Machærus and Herodias in the drawing-room; and that was not the worst of it, for there was Herod's soul, for which they were contending, resisting finally the pleadings of the prophet, and yielding to the seductions of an immodest girl, so that the adversity of the righteous did no good to anybody, and the prosperity of the wicked went on from harm to harm triumphantly, and made the cautious say, what profit is there in anything but evil ? The marvel of God's moral government grows, the perplexity of it only deepens.

6. And that illustration brings another unsolved problem—*the passing out of useful lives.* The prophet's head brought in on a charger—the lips dumb that had preached righteousness! Why should not good men last—longer, at any rate,

than they do? Useless waste, again, of talents, of education, of well-won influence. There are those among us—we may almost be excused for saying it—whom no one would miss; and there are those among us whom everybody would miss; and there have been those among us whom everybody does miss, so full of living power and usefulness were they; and these go first, and those linger longest. A great mystery and perplexity again!

7. And last, for I will not prolong the sorrowful recapitulation. It seems to me that there is no greater perplexity than this: *the difficulty there is in getting at the truth, in knowing what we are to believe and what we are to do.* If God has made a revelation, why has He not made it easy for us to understand it, and impossible for us to misunderstand it? Why has He not written out His will upon the heavens? Why do doubts, scientific and unscientific, arise in our hearts, obstructing our vision of God and blurring our dear conceptions of duty? A most distressing perplexity in these days, when the things we thought we believed we do not know whether we believe them or not. So many sonorous voices challenge this and so many challenge that, what is the bewildered soul to think or do?

All these perplexities are nothing new. You have felt them ever since you began to think, and almost whenever you do think. The only thing new about them, it may occur to you, is hearing them from the pulpit, which—perhaps you may have said to yourself—is greatly given to discussing things which everybody is not particularly thinking about, and nobody finds any difficulty in understanding. And perhaps you think that if the pulpit notices these real problems of life and thought, it is bound to explain them. Well, this pulpit at any rate is not going to try to explain them, simply because this pulpit knows that it cannot explain them.

And, moreover, it may be said in passing, that as the Christian religion did not create these difficulties, it is not bound to explain them. They are difficulties in nature, not in revelation. Every man feels every one of them, whether he is a Christian or not. If the Christian Church were extinguished to-day, men would still be struggling with questions such as these. All the Church can do is to alleviate, in some cases, the perplexities they cause, by opening a vision of other truths and other facts, which, we can dimly see, may possibly contain some helps towards their solution. The Church can impress you more strongly with the thought that in the life and immortality which are brought to light by the Gospel there may be opportunity to deal with the perplexities of this mortal life under more favorable conditions for finding their solution. But, after all, the difficulties will be felt so long as we are here, in spite of reason and revelation both.

What then? What is the conclusion these perplexing facts seem to point to? The conclusion is sometimes taken to be that, *God is not a Being Whom we can love and trust.* And, therefore, that we may as well be *godless.* That this world, with all its worries and perplexities, is all before us, and is the only thing that is before us. That there is no such thing as duty, because there is no motive to it, and no one to enforce it —there is only *inclination.* That there is no hope here, and none beyond; therefore, "Let us eat and drink, for to-morrow we die."

II. But *"God so loved the world that He gave His Only-begotten Son."* We confront all these unsolved problems of life with this simple statement. We are not going to try to solve them; but somewhere there is a solution not inconsistent with this fact, that "God sent His Son into the world." For what should He send His Son into the world, unless He cared for the world? Then the world is worth caring for. It is worth our caring for, and *life is worth living.* If He loves the world, then that makes a different thing of life in it from what it would be if God did not love the world. Face all these problems. Admit their difficulty. *But deny the inference that God is not a Being Whom we can love and trust.* On the contrary, take your stand on this fact of the Incarnation of the Son of God. It must make a difference in everything, so tremendous a fact. Believe it. *Believe it hard.* Never mind how you got to believe it. Because you grew up in that faith, thank God that you did grow up in it, and think it no shame that your soul was fed on positive beliefs rather than on innutritious negatives. If you have reasoned out sufficient reasons for believing the revelation—thank God for that. If, when you have tried to realize a world without a living and loving God, the drear was so dark and dismal that you could not endure it, then thank God that you could not. Thank God, anyhow, that you believe the Christian Gospel. It satisfies the heart, let the intellect flounder as it will, and better a bewildered intellect than an empty heart. Human nature without Christian faith is "an infant crying in the night"; faith takes hold of the Father's hand, and walks contented by His side through dark places, fearing nothing.

III. By the side of all these perplexities of natural religion, therefore, let us place this fact of revealed religion, the gift of God's Son to the world. It will not resolve the perplexities, *but it will dispose of them.* In the face of this fact, that God sent His Son into the world, it is impossible to believe that God is not a Being Whom we can love and trust, which is the conclusion to which those indisputable facts might lead us. And if we hold fast to the belief that God is a Being Whom we can love and trust, then nothing else need much trouble us. We will be still, and know that God is God, and that God is Love, and knowing, rest.

But, dear brethren, I know that there are trials of your faith, problems, perplexities, harder to bear than these comparatively abstract questions which I have used for illustration. The evil that is in you, and that you wot of, and that you have struggled with so hard—it is still there, a shame, and pain, and grief to you, and also a perplexity. Do not be persuaded into feeling that your struggle is vain, and that your evil will yet master you. Put this beside it in your thought—"*God so loved the world, loved me, that He gave His Only-begotten Son.*" He is God; be still, my fearful heart! A loving God, Whom I can love and trust; I yet will trust in Him!

And whatever the specific solutions of these several problems may be—the questions both abstract and personal which we have used for illustration there is this explanation of them as a whole, that they drive us upon trust in God, a trust in Him so absolute and entire, that no amount of perplexity can shake us out of it. This is evidently, if God is God, our true attitude toward Him. A child who challenges an explanation of all his father does, before he will accept it, is unnatural. The natural thing is that he should take things upon trust. But this implies that he is sure of his father—sure that he has knowledge and power, and that he cares paternally for him. And so it is not unreasonable that God should give to man, whom He would have to love and trust Him, some proof of His care and love for man which is absolute and overwhelming. In view of all these manifold perplexities—reasons for doubting God they seem to be, in themselves considered—there must be some one unchallengable reason for not doubting, but for trusting Him. This reason He has given—this firm ground of trust He has established in the Incarnation, life, and death of His Only-begotten Son. As we have followed the details of the story, it has grown vivid and real to our conception in the series of Christian fast and festival just ended for the year; it has not been announced simply that God became man; the fact has been dwelt upon and reiterated, and clothed with circumstance and detail which have not belittled it but have helped our minds to grasp it. It is the vastest, most awful and tremendous fact that can be conceived of, and such it must and ought to be if it is to have the effect upon us that it is needed for. To convince us in the midst of so many perplexities which this world presents, that God is a Being Whom we can love and trust, is not indeed, the only purpose of the Incarnation, but it is one purpose and one effect of it, and a worthy and valuable one; and it is impossible to conceive of a proof of God's love more convincing than this, that

"God so loved the world that He sent His Only-begotten Son."

To make life worth living, then, to dispose of its perplexities without solving them, two things are necessary. The first is, that we be sure that God is God—and that is a necessary and intuitive belief of unperverted minds. The second is, that we be assured that He loves the world; and this is proved by the gift of His Son. And if God so loved the world, then He loves me. And if God is God, then I must do His will; the inference is *Duty*. And if He loves me, then *Love* is the inference; I must love Him because He first loved me.

God grant us all grace, in this perplexing world, at least for *Love* and *Duty*. "Because, through the weakness of our mortal nature, we can do no good thing without Thee, grant us the help of Thy grace, that in keeping Thy commandments we may please Thee, both in will and deed; through Jesus Christ our Lord. Amen."

CHRIST THE FIRST-FRUITS.

EASTER DAY, S. JOHN'S, STAMFORD, APRIL 9, 1882.

CHRIST THE FIRST-FRUITS.

"Every man in his own order: Christ the first-fruits; afterward they that are Christ's at His coming."—I. CORINTHIANS XV. 23.

"On Good Friday, human nature, in the Person of its Representative, acknowledged its guilt, and yielded up its forfeited life. Yielded it up, that on Easter Day it might take it again. Human nature rose again in Christ—and that means that *the redemption and moral regeneration of mankind is to come through its close and corporate union with an omnipotent and perfect Moral Being, even with God Himself, in the Person of Jesus Christ.* Let us remember that the object of all religion is to unite man to God; to restore, rather, the broken unity. And this is what has been effected by Jesus Christ, Who took our nature upon Him, and gives to mankind of His glorified humanity. For we must have some community of nature with those we would love, *and what God wants, and we need, is love between us.*

In thinking of the Resurrection of Christ, therefore, we want to keep in mind not simply that it was *a Man* that rose, but *Man;* that as mankind suffered in Him, so it rose in Him. Every individual of the race did this, so far as

CHRIST THE FIRST-FRUITS.

he accepts Christ as his Representative, or, rather, does not refuse Him as such.

I wish that this idea of the representative character of the Man Christ Jesus could be so emphasized as that it should lie continually at the root of all our theological thinking. Perhaps it may be illustrated in part. When General Lee surrendered his sword to General Grant, the Southern Confederacy surrendered its sword, and every man in it, *so far as he did not repudiate what General Lee had done,* surrendered individually. Thenceforward the Southern people were united, re-united, with the nation, and the whole was regarded as a unit. In like manner mankind laid down its life in Christ, and thenceforward was regarded as having made atonement for its sin. In like manner, too, mankind is now regarded as having potentially risen again, and the individuals of the race claim their share in the benefits of this transaction by every act of faith which they put forth in their risen Lord and Head. And the reason we are left here on earth is that we may have opportunity, one by one, and each for himself, to put forth this act of faith, and to grow in faith, and get our hearts and wills more closely united to Him in Whom we spiritually live, and move, and have our immortal being. And by and by, if we work out our salvation on this plan, we shall be perfect moral beings, too—all the struggle ended, all the hindrances to a true life overcome.

That which hinders us now from a perfect moral life is the world, the flesh, and the devil. But in the future life the devil—all spiritual agents and agencies of evil—will be bound, and shall tempt the nations no more. And the world, *i. e.*, our associations and surroundings, will be such as to help, and not hinder, the best in us.

But on Easter Day it is natural to emphasize the hope we cherish of deliverance from the burden of the flesh. All in our present constitution which hinders the spirit will be put away, and left behind us in the grave. "O wretched man that I am," exclaimed the Apostle, after depicting the conflict between the natural man and the spiritual man in him, "who shall deliver me from this body of death?" And then he adds, "I thank God that I am delivered through Jesus Christ, our Lord." He was delivered in part, then, for while with the flesh he served the law of sin—he could not get the better of it entirely—yet with the mind, the spiritual part in him, his will, his conscience, his affections, he served the law of God. And what he longed for was to have the flesh so subdued to the spirit in him, that he should serve the law of God entirely.

To this he looks forward when he shall have a body perfectly fitted to the uses of the spirit. "There is a natural body," he says, "and there is a spiritual body." What does he mean by a spiritual body? He means just such a body as that in which Christ rose from the grave, in which He was for forty days upon the earth, and in which He ascended into heaven, and now sitteth at the right hand of God. And what was that Body? In some respects it was the same as before His death, and in some respects it was different. The same in its form and substance, but different in its qualities.

The same in its substance, certainly, for no part of it was left behind in the tomb of Joseph of Arimathea. It was not ethereal, but material, for He said, "A spirit hath not flesh and bones as ye see Me have." And evidently it was the same in form, for His disciples recognized Him after His Resurrection as they had done before. His features and the tones of His voice were unchanged. The marks of the nails and the spear remained upon Him. He retained His identity and the marks of identity. He recalled to their minds things that He had said to them in His previous life, and things they had done to Him (*e.g.* Peter). And yet, there was a difference. He comes and goes, not after the manner of mortal men. His disciples evidently felt the difference. The change in the qualities of His Body, which fitted it to ascend into heaven and continue there under conditions different from its conditions here, took place at its resurrection and at no other time. What the change was, and how effected we cannot tell.

And the Apostle clearly teaches that while the

resurrection of mankind is a reality, there is a difference between the bodies that go down into the grave and those that come forth from it. Identity—in whatever that consists—is not destroyed. Identity is not lost in the transfiguration of the seed to the flower, of the chrysalis to the butterfly. "To every seed *its own body.*" But the qualities are changed. If we knew what a particle of matter really is, we might perhaps form clearer notions of the change, but science has not yet got that far, and it is not safe to affirm or deny anything about it. But science does tell us that matter assumes very different forms and qualities as it is brought under the operation of different laws and forces.* Here we must rest our attempts at explanation—we can conceive that it may be, but we cannot show how it is. But as to the fact, there is no reason for doubting the Apostle's simple statement of it: "Flesh and blood cannot inherit the kingdom of God"; "It is sown a natural body; it is raised a spiritual body"; "There is a natural body, and

---

* "We are told by our scientific men that in the instant necessary to flash the electric spark from Europe to America, the molecules not only of 3000 miles of wire, but of the sheathing in which the wire is enclosed, and of the water in its immediate neighborhood, have either changed their place, or been affected somehow. There is undoubtedly the exertion of a new power. But how innumerable are the powers in the universe of which we yet know nothing ! We may not fully comprehend, but the analogies around us may at least bid us be silent."—Milligan, p. 20.

there is a spiritual body." We are told how we came by them: "The first Adam was made a living soul"—our mortal and fleshly life is derived from him; "The last Adam a life-giving spirit"—our spiritual and immortal life is derived from Him. There is no more difficulty about the latter than about the former. Both are the work of a Divine power.

We shall be relieved of some of our difficulty in conceiving of a spiritual world if we dismiss from our minds the idea that "spiritual" and "material" are opposites, and inconsistent with each other. We have no right to say they are. We should rather conceive of a state of things in which matter does not assert itself—has, so to speak, no will of its own, but lends itself unreservedly to the uses of spirit. We can understand, in a measure, how this may be, by thinking of some people in whom the spiritual element decidedly predominates over the material, whose bodies are not absolutely but very largely controlled by their spirits; while there are others of whom the reverse is true. Make the spirit absolutely dominant, and you have a spiritual body. A world adapted to such spiritual bodies would answer all our ideas of a spiritual world, *i. e.*, of heaven. I suppose it was some such temporary spiritualizing of our Lord's earthly body that took place in what we call the Transfiguration, when He, with Moses and Elias, appeared in a momentary revelation of the heavenly state to the eyes of the disciples. And if matter is to assume any shape at all for the uses of a spiritual body, it is certainly beyond our capacity to conceive any form more fit, more expressive, more adaptable to a glorious state of existence, than "the human form Divine."

There are several practical and helpful considerations, growing out of what has been said, to which I would briefly call your thoughts.

1. When we speak of Christ having our human nature, we are to think of Him as having not only our present weak humanity, but as having also our future and glorified humanity— we shall be one with Him in that, as we are in this. We are apt, I think, to dwell on the humanity of Christ as it was while He was on the earth; to take comfort, when we suffer, in remembering that He, too, suffered, "in all points like as we are." More helpful, still, will it be to remember that His Incarnation was perfected in His Resurrection, and that He is still the same, "the *Man* Christ Jesus." The weakness has become power; the natural body was sown, and has been raised a spiritual body; and He is as near to us as ever. "Christ the first-fruits," is now the glorified Man, "afterward they that are Christ's at His coming."

2. Another thought. What we are aiming at in this life is to subdue the flesh as much as possible to the spirit. We have small success, we often think, but we have some. It will help us

if we remember that while it is only begun here, yet the beginning holds the promise of completion when we shall have left behind us in the grave all the low and earthly part of our humanity, and we rise with bodies which not hinder but serve the spirit. Again, "Christ the first-fruits; afterward they that are Christ's at His coming."

3. Again, we shall know each other. There can be no doubt of that, if we believe that we shall be, after our resurrection, as Christ was after His. For His friends recognized Him; He looked at them out of the same eyes, and spoke to them with the same familiar voice, and they knew Him for the same, and recalled their common sympathies and experiences. And so shall we. "Christ the first-fruits; afterward they that are Christ's at His coming."

4. And, finally, light is thrown on the meaning of the Eucharist. The catechism asks, "What is the outward part or sign of the Lord's Supper?" And the answer is, "Bread and wine, which the Lord hath commanded to be received." "What is the inward part or thing signified?" "The Body and Blood of Christ, which are spiritually taken and received by the faithful in the Lord's Supper." That is to say, the Body that was broken and the Blood that was shed, just as the faithful Hebrews ate a part of the symbolic victim slain in sacrifice, of which the fire of God consumed the rest in token of their joint communion, so

we instead of that eat the symbols which He substituted for the old symbols of *the* Lamb of God, while the real thing of which we and they are made partakers is the humanity of Christ. And then the next question is, "What are the benefits whereof we are partakers thereby?" And the answer to that is, "The strengthening and refreshing of our souls by the Body and Blood of Christ, as our bodies are by the bread and wine." This means that, spiritually feeding on His *slain Body*, we are made partakers of His *risen and glorified humanity*. The life which is now His flows into us through this channel of His appointment, and we are united to Him now as the branches are united to the vine, and the living fluid flows out from Him into us, strengthening and refreshing our souls for the conflict we now are carrying on with evil, and which is to issue in the same triumph which He has Himself achieved. We are made partakers of that Spirit or life in Him which has already changed His Body from a natural to a spiritual body. Our Eucharistic communion with Him is a foretaste and pledge of our heavenly and spiritual life—a life in which spirit dominates body. "Christ the first-fruits; afterward they that are Christ's at His coming." This is the thought that underlies the administration of the sacrament of the dying, to prepare them for their end, to fortify them with the life that overcomes death. This is the thought that underlies the weekly communion, that on every Lord's Day, which is the weekly Easter, we should commune with and participate in our risen Lord. And this, too, gives its special significance to the Easter Eucharist, and marks the special privilege and duty of all Christians to commune with their risen Lord on the anniversary of His Resurrection to the new and immortal and perfectly spiritual life. With this faith, and the just expectation of benefit and blessing which springs out of this faith, let us approach His altar to-day. The bread and wine to be offered upon it are the memorial of His Body and Blood offered on the cross; the grace that will flow, through the partaking of them, into faithful souls is the grace of life which comes to us from the humanity of the Lord in glory. What He is, that, through His grace, we shall be. "Christ the first-fruits; afterward they that are Christ's at His coming."

LOOKING UP, AND NOT DOWN.

FOR LENT, S. JOHN'S, STAMFORD, MARCH 10, 1895.

LOOKING UP, AND NOT DOWN.

THE TRUE USES AND LIMITS OF SELF-EXAMINATION.

"My sins have taken such hold upon me, that I am not able to look up: yea, they are more in number than the hairs of my head, and my heart hath failed me."—PSALM xl. 15. (PRAYER BOOK.)

There are cases in which this lament of the Psalmist expresses, literally and absolutely, the condition of a sinful soul. "Tied and bound with the chain of our sins"—"the bands of these sins which by our frailty we have committed"—it is possible to become so satisfied with the bondage that even the desire for freedom is felt no more. Reprobate, not by any Divine decree, but by the acquiescence of the whole being in evil, the hope of being something better, and sometimes even the wish to be, which lingers long in every human soul seems at length to pass away. "My sins have taken such hold upon me that I am not able to look up"—this may be the expression of an utter and hopeless indifference to God and duty.

But on the lips of the Psalmist it is rather the expression of spiritual discontent. And so we may adopt it as our own—a confession of natural weariness and discouragement under sin, and in the failure to realize the Christian ideal. Of discouragement, but not of despair, for despair will never pray, as in the following verse: "O Lord, let it be Thy pleasure to deliver me ; make haste, O Lord, to help me." The heart is not logical nor careful about consistency in its expression of itself. In one breath a lament that it cannot look up to God, in the next, a looking up, a prayer for help and deliverance.

And now, albeit it is very needful always that we should have a very real sense of sin and a very deep penitence for it, let us take in the idea seemingly inconsistent therewith but really complementary to it: *That it is possible to dwell too much on our own sinfulness.*

Too much, that is, in relation to other spiritual facts, too exclusively, disproportionately. There are other things to be thought of ; we are not to dwell among the tombs perpetually; there is sunshine as well as shadow in the Christian life, and we are bidden to "walk in the light."

Perhaps we do not often think of the danger of excessive self-consciousness in religion. There are few of the modern manuals of devotion but what encourage this excess. And there are temperaments that come to delight in a morbid anatomy of themselves. They are full of self when they should be more and more empty of self. If they cannot find anything good to value themselves upon, they will contemplate their own spiritual unhealthiness, and take some

LOOKING UP, AND NOT DOWN.

strange satisfaction in that. They crave the luxury of excited feeling, and it is not always of very much importance how they get it. Witness the unhealthy self-reference, the often unblushing exaggeration of confession, in what are called "experience-meetings" where grief and shame for sin are not by any means too deep for words or tears.

Self-contemplation, beyond a certain point, is about as unprofitable and unsatisfactory an exercise as the Christian soul can well engage in. To the extent of ascertaining whether we are indeed living lives of faith and obedience, and doing all we can to get the better of our ill-tendencies, it is a right and necessary thing, and no Christian ought to live without it. But this legitimate use of self-examination ought not to be made to cover its abuse. The short, sharp, rigid self-scrutiny which seeks out the evils in one's character for the purpose of correcting them, and the weak points in order to strengthen them, should not be allowed to degenerate into the vague, listless, nerveless, unpractical self-contemplation that contents itself with the day dream of a better spiritual state, and lapses easily, though reluctantly, into the self-same lines of sinful thought, and feeling, and action, which it commenced by regretting. Have we never experienced this? Have we never sat down to take ourselves to task for some sin—we have fallen into it often, we seem to be no nearer overcoming it—what shall we do about it? And the thing is turned over in our mind, remorsefully at first, but by and by with a gentler sadness, until the vigorous and healthy self-condemnation subsides into a sort of self-pity for those constitutional tendencies which it is so hard to eradicate, and those unpropitious circumstances which restrain our better aspirations. If we would let self-examination work out some practical result in the way of self-discipline, and turn our griefs to some purpose, it would be a great deal better for us. "Wherefore liest thou thus upon thy face?" said the Lord to Joshua; "get thee up and put away the accursed thing." Self-discipline, in some form or other, is a test and expression to ourselves of the sincerity of our dissatisfaction with what we find within us. Fasting for a sin will be much more to the purpose than grieving over it, on the principle that a feeling is strengthened always by being embodied in an act. And if it is difficult, for any reason, to discipline ourselves, then there is all the more reason for doing it. There is nothing that can rescue a life from the misery of being misgoverned by a nerveless, inefficient will.

And as self-discipline should be the practical result of self-examination on the one hand, so prayer should be its practical result on the other. "This kind goeth not out by prayer and fasting." I commend this Lenten philosophy of our Lord's teaching to the many men who are in peril of intemperance, and, indeed, of every sensual sin. What shall I do with these tendencies and temptations which beset me? "I keep under my body, and bring it into subjection." "I will lift up mine eyes unto the hills from whence cometh my help." "My help cometh from the Lord, Who hath made heaven and earth." To rise out of discouragement into trust again, out of the darkness and despondency that comes of looking on the past, where the most apparent thing is failure, and to look with hope to the promises of grace which light up the future. And if for a moment we give way to the weariness of disappointment, and say, "My sins have taken such hold upon me that I am not able to look up," if prayer itself seems a hopeless and a futile thing, as it often will, still the very act of prayer will bring back the spirit of prayer. It is my only hope—the heart will say—if I give up this I give up everything, for I have no other resource. It seems to bring me but little good, but it is the only thing that brings me any. I pray in the closet, "Lead me not into temptation, But deliver me from evil"—and straightway I go into the world and encounter the evil, or I remain at home, and temptation comes to me. I have prayed often, very often, against my sins, but their bands appear to be as strong as ever. I am weary and sick at heart with desires ineffective, and purposes unfulfilled. But what can I do except that which I have done—pray yet again my seemingly unanswered prayer; rise up again after my many falls, and refuse to give up my trust in God. For, after all, why should I expect an easy victory, or that life should ever be an ended struggle? Can so great a result be accomplished by a wish? Nay, I will contend with my inward evil to the very end. "My sins are more in number than the hairs of my head, and my heart hath failed me." "But God is the strength of my heart, and my portion forever." "Lord, to whom shall I go but unto Thee? Thou hast the words of eternal life"—is the cry of the soul when, in its worst discouragement, it contemplates the alternative of giving up its hold on God.

For this would be just what Satan would desire. Sin has never done its worst work in us until it has clouded our trust in God. When it has so steeped us in distress, and doubt, and discouragement, and so thoroughly taken away all heart and hope that we are ready to give up what seems a useless struggle, then, indeed, however small a matter may be the occasion, it is deadlier in its results than ten thousand graver sins into which we fall, and out of which we rise again.

It is in this way that it becomes possible to dwell too much in thoughts of our own sinfulness. Hope and confidence are better allies in fighting any battle than doubtfulness and distrust. It is well to know the weak points, and

LOOKING UP, AND NOT DOWN.

to guard them; it is better, still, to know the strong ones, and rely upon them. And the weak point in all of us is looking too much at ourselves, *our* failures and *our* successes, for if the one may lead to undue self-reliance sometimes, the other may lead to distrust of God. Our strong point is trust, and reliance on supernatural, Divine grace, for "this is the victory that overcometh, even our faith."

In illustration of what has been said, let us notice how small a part confession of sin bears in our Church service. It is an essential thing in every approach of the sinner to God, and it comes in at the very beginning of our ritual, significantly, for it marks the fact that not until we recognize and acknowledge our transgressions are we fitted to come into His presence. We take an attitude of conscious unworthiness, befitting those whose first plea must ever be for mercy. But the confession itself is short, and deep, and strong, and then, throughout the service, there is no more of it. Sin is put out of the way ; God's ready forgiveness of the penitent is declared in the Absolution ; and why then should we longer dwell upon it ? We have something brighter and cheerier to look at in the reconciled face of Him to Whom we come, like children whose trembling approach in penitence has been welcomed, and say again, "Our Father, Who art in heaven." And then we praise, and then we listen to instruction for our future duty, and then we pray for grace to do it.

And so the right use of a consciousness of sin —which is, after all, largely a consciousness of weakness—is to lead us to *look up, and not down*. It is not an end in itself; we are none the better for knowing that we are bad, unless that knowledge leads us onward to something else. Self-examination is simply the probing of a wound, the diagnosis of a disease, preliminary to taking measures for its cure. "They that be whole need not a physician"; they that think themselves whole will not seek one. But they whose self-scrutiny discloses their spiritual unhealthiness had better not dwell very long on a fact which holds for them nothing but discouragement. The Israelites, bitten by the fiery serpents in the wilderness, might have looked upon the inflamed and festering flesh until they died. Naaman the Syrian might have examined his bleached and scaling skin for many a year, and it would have been bleached and scaling still. And so for us, "by the law is the knowledge of sin"; but by the law is no salvation from it. It is "our schoolmaster to bring us to Christ." He is the Fountain opened for sin and for uncleanness, and invites us to wash and be clean. He is lifted up, "as Moses lifted up the serpent in the wilderness," to be looked to for deliverance. "I, if I be lifted up, will draw all men unto Me"—away from their sin and unto

LOOKING UP, AND NOT DOWN.

Me, their Saviour. There is power in the accepted and realized thought of a free salvation which we have none of us yet sufficiently tried —motive power; motive and inducement and spiritual vigor for holiness of purpose and life in looking upon the Redeemer's cross, and beyond it upon the Father's forgiving love.

And instead of thinking altogether of our failures, let us think sometimes of the spiritual successes we have had. Where have they come from? No honest Christian life, however imperfect, is altogether a failure. You discouraged soul! you have not yielded to every temptation that has assailed you. You, who feel so far from God, have had hours of Divine communion. You have done some good in the world, and fulfilled some part of your duty to God as well as to man. You are not lost to sense of spiritual things; you have your aspirations. How have they come? No merit to yourself for all this; no cause for self-gratulation. Yet surely a cause for thanksgiving, and a ground for hope. "By the grace of God you are what you are." *And there is more where that came from.* Surely, a more satisfactory, more comforting, more helpful line of thought, and holding more of healthy inspiration for the future! When you have humbled yourself before God in view of what you have left undone, then rise up and thank Him for what He has done in you.

And so another most helpful and elevating

element in our devotions is *adoration*—worship, strictly so-called. As confession grows out of thinking about ourselves as we are, so adoration grows out of thinking of God as He is. *It is pure praise.* It differs from thanksgiving, which arises on the view of *what God is to us*, in this, that *it arises on the view of what He is in Himself.*

In these two elements of devotion, praise and thanksgiving, which form so large a part of our Church service, we shall find more help than from allowing the consciousness of personal sinfulness to take too much hold upon us, or too exclusive, so that we are not able to look up when our hearts have failed us so. For in the character and attributes of the God whom we adore, we find encouragement to trust and hope in Him. And in the many instances in which His grace has been our help already, we have an earnest of what will be in the future. The confession is a very necessary part of worship, but there is more of uplifting hope and strength and inspiration for duty in the Te Deum. And the Eucharist to which we are now and every Lord's Day invited, while it is prepared for by confession and absolution, is in its essence *a service of Thanksgiving.* Our Lenten days should ever be brightened with light thrown back upon them from Easter and Whitsun-tide.

GLORYING IN THE CROSS OF CHRIST.

EPISTLE, FIFTEENTH SUNDAY AFTER TRINITY, S. JOHN'S, STAMFORD, SEPTEMBER 22, 1895.

GLORYING IN THE CROSS OF CHRIST.

"God forbid that I should glory, save in the cross of our Lord Jesus Christ, by Whom the world is crucified unto me, and I unto the world. For in Christ Jesus neither circumcision availeth any thing, nor uncircumcision, but a new creature."—GALATIANS vi. 14, 15.

It was usual with St. Paul to write his letters—those which we call the epistles to the churches—by the hand of an amanuensis. They were, as we say now, "dictated." For example, the epistle to the Romans which begins, "Paul, a servant of Jesus Christ, called to be an Apostle," ends with the signature of his secretary. "I Tertius, who wrote this epistle, salute you in the Lord." Usually the Apostle appends his own signature, as at the end of the second epistle to the Thessalonians, " The salutation of Paul, with mine own hand, which is the token in every epistle: so I write."

And in this letter to the Galatians I think we may find a hint of the explanation of this habit of his. We have all observed, probably, that he often alludes to some bodily infirmity, which troubles him chiefly because to some extent it hinders his efficiency in work. He calls it "a thorn in the flesh, a messenger of Satan sent to buffet him." He speaks of his " bodily presence being called weak and his speech contemptible." (II. Cor. x. 10.) And again he "takes pleasure in his infirmities," when he remembers how the strength of God is made perfect in his own weakness. (II. Cor. xii. 9.) In this epistle to the Galatians he refers to it again. "Ye know how through infirmity of the flesh, I preached the gospel unto you at the first: and my temptation which was in my flesh ye despised not, nor rejected, but received me as a messenger of God." And then he adds these remarkable words; "I bear you record, that, if it had been possible, ye would have plucked out your own eyes and have given them to me." (iv. 15.) Now what can be inferred from this strong expression about giving him their eyes, but that there was something the matter with his, in other words, that St. Paul's bodily infirmity was some conspicuous disfigurement and distressing infirmity of sight which vexed and hindered his active spirit, and was a trial to him every day of his life, which his opponents sometimes threw up at him, which made it necessary that he should always travel in company with some one, and rendered Luke the Physician an especially suitable companion and helper ; which compelled him to carry on his correspondence mainly by the hands of a secretary, only the signature and a few words in conclusion being written by himself; and which gives meaning and emphasis to the closing words of this very epistle to the Galatians,

GLORYING IN THE CROSS OF CHRIST.

when he takes up the pen himself and emphatically re-affirms with his own hand the main sentiment of the whole letter. For the substance of what he says is not, "Ye see how large or long a letter," but "in what large letters." "Ye see by these big and scrawling letters in which I am now writing to you with my own hand how much in earnest I am, that it is my very self, your own true friend and apostle, who says these few words to you in conclusion." And perhaps he may refer to the origin of this partial blindness when he says in closing: "From henceforth let no man reproach me with it, for I bear in my body the marks of the Lord Jesus—marks which were forever stamped upon me in that blinding vision which arrested me in my opposition to my Lord when I was on the way to Damascus. But though it be my infirmity, it is, nevertheless my honor and not my shame!"

This glimpse of the struggle of a great soul with its bodily limitations is very pathetic, and full of instruction and comfort to many who would do more than they can for others and for God. St. Paul did his work under difficulties, but—*he did it*.

And now what was it that stirred up St. Paul to take his pen in hand in this impulsive and passionate way? It was that certain persons had undertaken to weaken his people's confidence in him, and especially in the truth which he had taught them. He had human nature enough, no doubt, to resent the personal slight, for the best men can be most deeply wounded through their affections. But it was still more intolerable that the doctrine of Christ, which he had taught them with such labor and pains, should be undermined. St. Paul's churchmanship was broad and high. The Christian Church was *The Church* for him, and not an appendage to the Jewish. There was another party in the Church even at that time which was in reality low and narrow, though they would call themselves High Churchmen. It was that party which insisted that the Christian Church was an offshoot from the Jewish, and therefore that the Jewish rites and observances were binding upon Christians still; who encumbered Christian worship with just as much of the old ceremonial as they could get in, and restricted Christian liberty with obsolete rules and rubrics, and took the very life out of Christian faith and love by insisting that men were justified not by spiritual union with Christ, but by their observance of the Old Law. Listen to his hot indignation as he repels this false teaching, remembering that what it really meant was that these plain and simple Gentile folk, descended from the wild Gallic tribes, whom the Roman legions had subdued and made peaceful citizens of a province in Asia Minor—that these simple converts of his from mere heathenism to Christianity, must become Jews before they could be real Christians. Just

GLORYING IN THE CROSS OF CHRIST.

as some in our day would have us adopt the cast-off doctrines and ceremonies of Romanism before we can be called good Churchmen—we, Anglo-Saxon Christians, who never were Romanists at all, or in any sense, except by compulsion for a brief period, and never will be again. "O foolish Galatians," he exclaims; "who hath bewitched you, that ye should not obey the truth, before whose eyes Jesus Christ hath been evidently set forth, crucified among you?" You know by inward experience that you have the Holy Spirit in you, helping you to better lives, to happiness, to spiritual power and freedom—"Received ye the Spirit by the works of the law, or by the hearing of faith? Having begun in the Spirit, are ye now made perfect by the flesh? Know ye that they which are of faith, they are the true children of Abraham. . . . But that no man is justified by the law is evident, for the just shall live by faith. And the law is not of faith," but was a covenant of works, and "Christ hath redeemed us from the curse of the law, being made a curse for us, . . . that the blessing of Abraham might come on the Gentiles through Jesus Christ; that we might receive the promise of the Spirit through faith"; and faith, with St. Paul, is just *an absolute and simple trusting of ourselves to the redeeming Christ.* The law has served its turn, has had its day, and we, he says, are living under the Gospel. "Ye are all the children of

God by faith in Jesus Christ, for as many as are baptized into Christ have put on Christ. There is now neither Jew nor Greek, for ye are all one in Christ Jesus." (Gal. iii.) Then he goes on to speak of the glory and the joy of the believing Christian, and asks, in righteous sarcasm, "How turn ye again to the weak and beggarly elements, whereunto ye desire again to be in bondage? Ye observe days, and months, and times, and years, making these things the essence of religion, not its helps," just as the old Jews did in the times of their training for better things. "I am afraid of you," he says, "lest I have bestowed on you labor in vain." And then he recalls pathetically his unselfish labors and sufferings in their behalf, and contrasts his spirit with the partisan spirit of those who would bring his work to naught. And so he goes on through the epistle, sometimes arguing, sometimes entreating, intensely personal, warmly loving, denouncing the false teachers, warning his converts of the dangers and temptations which the mere legal religion which was being imposed upon them would supply them with no strength to resist. And at last he pushes his secretary aside and seizes the pen with his own hand and scrawls a few closing lines to expose the motives of these emissaries of the Judaizing party, showing how they are only desirous "to make a fair show in the flesh," to get credit for their party by constraining these converts to be circumcised, while at the same time they themselves only keep the Jewish law in part. "But God forbid that I should glory," he exclaims, vehemently, "save in the cross of our Lord Jesus Christ, by which the world is crucified unto me, and I unto the world. For in Christ Jesus neither circumcision availeth anything, nor uncircumcision, but a new creature."

This is a strong expression about glorying in the cross of Christ. But not too strong for the glowing spirit of the Apostle, and not too strong for us, if we only take in what the cross of Christ stands for.

It stands, in the first place, for *the highest expression of God's love for man.* "God commendeth His love toward us, in that while we were yet sinners, Christ died for the ungodly.' "God spared not His own Son, but delivered Him up for us all." Love unfathomable—that is the key to all this universe of unfathomable things, making all intelligible in the light of a Divine purpose.

It stands, in the second place, for *the highest sacrificial expression of human brotherhood.* On the cross of Christ, suffering for others was made for the first time, and in the highest degree, the law of human life, and not its exception—suffering not for *some* others who are in relation to us, as our family and friends, which might be regarded simply as a noble manifestation of what is sometimes called "the larger selfishness," but suffering for *all* others—enemies as well as friends, the indifferent as well as the related. *Christ the Supreme Sufferer in a suffering world*—the Sufferer Whose suffering has alleviated and ennobled suffering, if not explained it, for us all who "suffer with Him."

It stands, in the third place, for *victory over evil*. The bruising of the heel of Christ was the bruising of the serpent's head. Nothing that ever happened was a more signal victory wrought out of apparent defeat; nothing, like the Crucifixion, has brought moral heroism and strength to mankind. *The triumph of Goodness.*

For the cross stands, finally, for *absolute self-consecration and absolute trust in God.* He who taketh not up his own cross, whatever it be, cannot be Christ's disciple. "Not my will, but Thine be done" has been translated since then into the supreme human motive—*Man, a "new creature."*

The glory of the cross, in all these aspects, is the glory that excelleth. "Till Jesus hung on it, the cross was the symbol of slavery and vulgar wickedness; but He converted it into the symbol of heroism, self-sacrifice, and salvation. Since then the world has gloried in it"—all that is noble and good in the world at least; "it has been carved in every form of beauty and every substance of price; it has been emblazoned on the flags of nations and engraved on the sceptres and diadems of kings. The cross was planted

GLORYING IN THE CROSS OF CHRIST.

on Golgotha a dry, dead tree; but, lo! it has blossomed like Aaron's rod; it has struck its roots deep down to the heart of the world, and sent its branches upwards, till to-day it fills the earth, and the nations rest beneath its shadow and eat of its pleasant fruits"—(Stalker, "Trial and Death of Jesus Christ," p. 167).

Here, then, was the glorious Gospel that the glorious Apostle gloried in—not an outward conformity to mere laws of life, not a formal membership in the visible Church; neither good morals nor ecclesiastical position began to touch the true inward and spiritual realities of Christ's religion, but that utter surrender and making over of the whole man through union of heart and soul with Christ crucified which made the true Christian indeed a new creature in Christ Jesus, which filled him with a new and bounding life, so that henceforth the world, its maxims and principles, its approbations and its rewards, were no more to him than as if he were a dead man. Yea, St. Paul *was* dead to the world, even as if he had been literally crucified with Christ, or as if the world itself had been crucified so far as he was concerned, so powerless was it with him. "Yea," he says, in a previous verse, "I am crucified with Christ, nevertheless I live; yet not I, but Christ liveth in me; and the life which I now live in the flesh, I live by the faith of the Son of God, who loved me, and gave Himself for me. And I do not frustrate the grace of God; for if righteousness came by the law, then Christ is dead in vain." (ii. 20, 21.)

This absolute and passionate trust in Christ, and utter devotion and submission to Him, has been the strength and inspiration of God's strong and masterful saints who have done great things for Him and for mankind in every age. Listen to some words of St. Francis of Assisi just before his death. "Let us all, with all our heart and all our thought, and all our strength, and all our mind, with all our vigor, with all our effort, with all our affection, with all our inward powers, our desires, and our wills, love the Lord God, who has given to us all His Body, all His Soul, all His Life, and still gives them every day to each of us. He created us, He saves us by His grace alone; He has been, He still is, full of goodness to us, us wicked and worthless, corrupt and ungrateful, ignorant, bad. We desire nothing else, we wish for nothing else ; may nothing else please us or have any attraction for us, except the Creator, the Redeemer, the Saviour, sole and true God, Who is full of goodness, Who is all goodness, Who is the true and supreme Good, Who alone is holy, righteous, true, upright, Who alone has benignity, innocence, and purity; of Whom, by Whom, and in Whom, is all the pardon, all the grace, all the glory of all penitents, of all the righteous and all the Sa nts who are rejoicing in heaven." (Life, p. 257.)

Brethren! if this, and all that it stands for, sounds remote from our average thought and experience, yet let us remember that it is after all the simple truth and substance of all inward and spiritual religion, and not try to bring down the Christian's standard of utter trust and devotion to our own actual level, but rather raise ourselves toward it even if we cannot get up to it. How very human are these Saints after all! How very human, especially, is St. Paul himself, who gives himself up so utterly to his Master, and consciously reserves nothing from Him, and who yet is so very natural withal! Who of us can feel that indeed we glory only in the cross of Christ, and that by it the world is crucified unto us, and we unto the world? And yet we ought to recognize this high Christian standard of inward experience, and sometimes indeed we do recognize it and seem to approach it in hours of strong aspiration. Yes, and Christians do good into it in large measure by long-continued faithfulness in duty, and by constant contemplation of the higher things, with conscious purpose drawing near to Christ and realizing their oneness with Him.

The prophet Jeremiah (ix. 23, 24) has a passage which reminds us of these words of St. Paul. "Thus saith the Lord, Let not the wise man glory in his wisdom, neither let the mighty man glory in his might, let not the rich man glory in his riches: But let him that glorieth glory in this, that he understandeth and knoweth Me, that I am the Lord which exercise lovingkindness, judgment, and righteousness in the earth: for in these things I delight, saith the Lord." This, indeed, is the true standard of satisfactoriness to the man of spiritual mind, the knowledge, the sympathetic knowledge of the righteous God. That he walks with Him, that he thinks with Him, that he feels with Him, that the high standards of God, which are the moral law of the universe, are his standards, and the low standards of earth are not his—that he is in touch of sympathy with all the highest and best things, with goodness, rather than with learning, greatness, and wealth. St. Paul Christianizes this thought; he glories in the cross of Christ, symbol of all that the world and the natural man rejects and despises. These low motives, these material successes, they are nothing to him—no more to him than they were to Jesus hanging on the tree. What he wanted for himself, and what he wants for his beloved Christian converts is, that they should all be made over, made new creatures in Christ Jesus, with all that is low and earthly in them subordinated to the higher spiritual life.

This is the standard which the great Apostle holds up before us. Let us not find our satisfactions in self, our character, our attainments, our successes, personal or partisan, but simply and solely in our union with Christ, that in Him we are new and different beings from our natural selves. In this is our comfort and satisfaction, in this our glory and joy, that we are one with Him in thought and feeling, knit together with Him in love and sympathy, and with all that is His because it is His. There is no credit to ourselves in this; He has taken us and made us over into His likeness and character. We are baptized into Christ, our life is tied with Christ in God. Neither circumcision availeth anything, nor baptism in itself, and outwardly, availeth anything—not our formal membership in the Church is the great thing, but the inward grace of God which the Church ministers to us, the life which circulates through His Body, the Church, and into all its faithful members—the sap which flows through the vine and into the branches, bringing forth much fruit.

Personal devotion to Christ crucified, in other words, *personal religion*—this is what we want—the affections of the devout heart, duty done out of a holy obedience, worship rendered out of love and reverence, a faith which controls, a motive which inspires us, the fruits of the Spirit here, and a hope full of immortality.

MAN'S NEED OF THE DIVINE TRINITY.

TRINITY SUNDAY, S. JOHN'S, STAMFORD, JUNE 20, 1886.

MAN'S NEED OF THE DIVINE TRINITY.

"Holy, holy, holy, Lord God Almighty, which was, and is, and is to come."—REV. iv. 8.

The teaching of the Church on Trinity Sunday has reference directly to the nature of God. We think of Him then as He is in Himself—going back of His relations to us in the detail in which they are set forth through all the course of the Christian year, and resting in the thought of the Supreme Being as He dwells in the Light unapproachable, with all the orders of superior spirits surrounding His throne, and crying "Holy, holy, holy." The first chapter of Genesis introduces Him as the Eternal One, Creator of the heavens and the earth, and from that point the Bible starts, and carries us along through His practical revelation of Himself to the spiritual needs of men.

It is here, then, that we most feel our need of a revelation. The first necessity of our nature is to know that we have a God; and then, how we are to conceive of Him; and then, what relation He holds to us, and how we are to realize for our own part our true relation to Him.

It is difficult to organize our thought of God. If we had no revelation from Himself of Himself it would be impossible; we could never "by searching find out God." The diligent student of evolution takes the ascertained facts of nature and of life, and works backward through all the operations of secondary laws and forces, until he comes at last to the Primal Force, and there he stops. What that is, he cannot tell—whether it is an intelligent Force, a Will, in other words, a Person, he cannot determine by those methods of investigation which have carried him back that far. The "natural man," St. Paul tells him, cannot know "the things of God, because they are spiritually discerned." The matter and the forces of the universe he can measurably understand, but the Divine Spirit in the universe he cannot get to understand by the light of science. "What man knoweth the things of a man, save the spirit of man which is in him? Even so the things of God knoweth no man, but the Spirit of God." But though man cannot find God, *yet God can find man*—can reveal Himself to him, can enlighten him with sufficient knowledge of Himself. Such knowledge is communicated through the spiritual faculty in man, in respect of which he is in the image of God. For, St. Paul adds, "we have received, not the spirit of the world, but *the Spirit* which is of God, that we might know the things which are freely given to us of God."

The spiritual faculty through which we must get the touch of God is *faith*. We are guided by science, which means knowledge, through the regions of sense, but we come to the end of all that long and wonderful way of nature and as to what is beyond, we are all *agnostics*, until God takes us by the hand and carries us into still higher regions of thought and feeling. He reveals Himself in His spiritual relations to us with as much certainty as in His natural laws He reveals His natural government of us and all around us. I know that, to very many, faith seems only another word for uncertainty. That is because they fail to recognize the distinct and separate uses of the spiritual and the natural faculties, *and that certainty can come through both.* Science is the solid tread of the feet upon the ground. Faith is the flight of the bird. It springs from its footing on the church tower, it falls a space, poises itself, springs upward, and cleaves the trackless spaces of the air, as safely, confidently, and as much in accordance with the laws and methods of its own being, as does the plodder on the surface of the earth with the methods and laws of his being. Faith is the wing of the soul—it is in its element in the spiritual region, as science is in the natural region; to keep the soul down to things of earth is to cage it, to limit its freedom and its joy. Now, God's revelation of Himself is made to faith; it is His call to the soul to come up higher, to breathe His atmosphere, to move in celestial scenes, to aspire, to make excursions from material surroundings and conditions from time to time, and to dwell in Him and with Him, in Whose image it was made.

The soul of man desires God, and is hungry till it find Him. "Thou hast made us for Thee," says St. Augustine, "and our heart is unquiet till it rest in Thee." Agnosticism is no resting-place for the human spirit. The soul goes back, and back, to the beginning, and is not content so long as there is only a query, an unknown, at the end of its search. But the first words of the Bible satisfy: "In the beginning—God."

A few verses on, and we find the origin of man, made in the intellectual and moral image of God; inspired with the breath of life he became—whatever in the fancy of the evolutionist he may have been before—he then and so became "worthy to be called a man," when God "breathed into his nostrils the breath of life, and man became a living soul."

From what man knows himself to be, he infers what God is. For if man is in the image of God, then God must be in the image of man. The two must fit and correspond to each other.

The Christian teaching of the threefold personality of God answers to the needs of human nature. There is mystery in it. We cannot fully organize our thought about it so as to satisfy the logical habit of mind which is characteristic of our day. But it satisfies the spiritual imagina-

MAN'S NEED OF THE DIVINE TRINITY.

tion, and affords a practical basis for religious thought and life.

"First, I learn to believe in God the Father, Who hath made me and all the world.

"Secondly, in God the Son, Who hath redeemed me and all mankind.

"Thirdly, in God the Holy Ghost, Who sanctifieth me and all the people of God."

1. God is, first of all, a Father. We need, yea, we crave to feel Him such.

For the first element in the idea of fatherhood is *authority*, and the answering obedience of childhood. Human nature owns a superior—it cries out for a law and a lawgiver. It knows it is responsible and accountable to some one. The independence which it foolishly seeks so often, in its wiser and better moments it disowns. It takes in naturally the idea that it is a child of God, and then begins to learn the Ten Commandments. "Thou shalt have none other gods but Me," and then on that follow the details of duty.

The second element in the idea of fatherhood is *love*. God is not *a mere Lawgiver*. That would not satisfy. We have a heart, and the demand of the heart is imperative for a supreme and altogether worthy object of affection. No earthly thing can satisfy that craving. Self cannot satisfy it. Self-love eats out the heart that has no larger love. "God is love, and he that dwelleth in love dwelleth in God, and God in him."

The third element in the idea of fatherhood is *care*—provision for the needs of the child. That is the *providence* of God. We crave the assurance of it—that we are not left unprovided and uncared for—orphans in a cold, unsympathizing world of laws and forces. That the hairs of our head are numbered, that we can ask for daily bread, that our life is on a plan, and not a series of accidents or a chain of remorseless consequences, that we are in training for a future. All this we crave to know; and because God is our Father, we know it, and are content.

"Secondly, in God the Son, Who hath redeemed me and all mankind."

The doctrine of a Saviour answers to the needs of men. The relations of the Divine Son to the Father we conceive with difficulty. But the relations of the Divine Saviour to human sinners presents no difficulty. For we know good and evil, and that evil dwells in us we know too well. How to be saved from it we desire to know. And the revelation in Scripture tells us.

It reveals the Incarnation. And the Incarnation—the indwelling of God in human nature—is an idea so natural as to be almost necessary. The idea of a Divine Being entering into human flesh and form is so natural that in some form or other it has always been part of the religious thought of mankind.

The consciousness of sin is a fact in human experience, and it is worthy of such a Divine interposition as the Scripture reveals to deliver mankind from it. Sin means alienation from a good God, and the active presence of God in us means deliverance from sin. Where one is, the other cannot long be. And whenever we are conscious of a desire for goodness, it is the indication of the struggle of that Diviner element which Christ has imparted into our nature with the evil that has somehow got there. The conflict is unceasing. The Christ in us is saying, "Sin shall not have dominion over you." And if that is our will, also our choice, then it shall not. The stronger shall cast out the strong. His name is Emmanuel—God with us. This is the meaning of the Incarnation.

In like manner the Atonement is a necessary and natural idea. Its meaning is deliverance from the guilt of sin. That can only be received by sacrifice, and sacrifice is an idea that has always been present to the thought of man in his relation with God. He who is so united with us as to be *the man*—the Representative Man—acknowledged human guilt, and atoned for it. Not in behalf of an arbitrarily selected few, nor yet in behalf of those only who would accept His action for them, but for all mankind He died, and in dying made atonement for every human soul.

And so now the breach between God and man

is healed, and the way is open for every child of God to come into his Father's presence and claim his heritage of love. God the Saviour—this conception of the second Person in the Blessed Trinity answers to human needs.

"Thirdly, in God the Holy Ghost, Who sanctifieth me and all the people of God."

Philosophers find no difficulty in conceiving of a force pervading the world—dwelling latent in inanimate things, but there and ready to be awakened, or else active in beings that live. Such a force, pervading human nature, and dwelling in each human soul, is the Christian conception of the Holy Spirit of God. The Author of every moral movement in the individual or in society, the Inspirer of every good affection, "the Lord and the Giver of Life."

We are taught to conceive of the Holy Ghost as God the Sanctifier. Conscious of sin, and accepting pardon, our hope of deliverance from it lies in the continual presence with our spirits of a Divine Helper. We have no confidence in ourselves—our future will be but a progress in evil unless we have spiritual strength given to us from above. Light and power, teaching and help, "that we may both perceive and know what things we ought to do, and also may have grace and power faithfully to perform the same" —this is the spiritual need of man.

This need is met by the revelation of the third Person in the Blessed Trinity, dwelling in our individual souls, and dwelling in the Church.

We are conscious of continual conflict going on within us, between our lower and our higher natures—the one drawing us downward, and the other drawing us upward, all the time. We need continual re-enforcement of our higher life, from God, the Source of life—continually fresh supplies of grace. We receive it, through continual infusions of the Divine Spirit into hearts that open themselves to receive them. As life and death are in continual conflict in the natural world, waste and repair going on unceasingly, so in the moral and spiritual world of each individual soul the same conflict goes on, and we are in perpetual flux between the death of sin and the life of righteousness, God, the Life giver, repairing the waste of our moral tissues, lest sin and death claim us for their own.

The same thing goes on, on larger scale, in society, and the Holy Ghost is the life of the Church. The use of the Church is to be, as it were, a world within a world, to surround us with a spiritual atmosphere, so that, as the world helps the evil in us, the Church may help the good, bringing breezes of purer air, in which our souls may be refreshed, and provisions of spiritual food by which they may be nourished. Take away the Christian Church from its place in the world—abolish its Sundays, suspend its worship, arrest its teachings, stop the flow of grace through its channels of grace, take away the mutual help and countenance in right-doing which its members afford to one another, and the struggle of the individual soul with its individual temptations becomes hopeless. Or, let the Church become dead, while retaining the form and organization of life, so that its functions cease, so that it ceases to help the individual soul in its struggles with the evil in it, and in the world, and then sin and death will resume their dominion over us and over society. This large conception of the office of the Holy Spirit in the Church and in the world is a worthy and satisfying one—worthy of God, and satisfying to human needs.

The Gospel for Trinity Sunday is the fit sequence to the first lesson. The one records the creation of the earth and of man—the Spirit of God moving on the face of the chaotic deep, and imparting orderly force for the organizing and shaping of the natural world, and then breathed into man's nostrils to make him a living soul. The other records the method of man's regeneration—the new-birth of water and the Holy Ghost, the revivifying of what was dead in sin, the renewal of the defaced image of God in righteousness and true holiness, and the gathering in of living souls into the ordered kingdom of heaven.

Let this be the conception of God in His nature, gathered from the consideration of His threefold relation to us, as Father, Saviour, Sanctifier, which we take away with us on this Trinity Sunday. We may not, as was said, be able to organize our thought on the subject of the relations of the Three Divine Persons in the One Godhead each to the other. But we can take in their relations to us. The Father, ruling, loving, providing. The Son, sharing our human nature, lifting it up into the Divine, and bringing us into peace and reconciliation with God. The Holy Spirit, a regenerating and strengthening spiritual Force in us, in the Church, and in the world. Let us not think about the Trinity speculatively, but practically. Then we shall join, with mind and heart alike, in the Church's offering of pure praise, "Holy, holy, holy!"

GOD'S SEEKING THE SINNER.

SECOND LESSON, EIGHTEENTH SUNDAY AFTER TRINITY, S. JOHN'S, STAMFORD, OCTOBER 1, 1893.

GOD'S SEEKING THE SINNER.

"What man of you, having a hundred sheep, if he lose one of them, doth not leave the ninety and nine in the wilderness, and go after that which is lost, until he find it?"—ST. LUKE XV. 4.

It is by no mere accident of discourse that the three parables—of the Lost Sheep, of the Lost Piece of Money, and of the Prodigal Son—are brought together in our Lord's teaching, as we have it in the second lesson for to-day. They all refer to one subject—looked at from different points of view. The one subject is: the coming together of God and the soul, after they have been set apart by sin. And the difference in the points of view is mainly this: that in the parables of the Lost Sheep and the Lost Piece of Money, the thought is of God's seeking man, while in the parable of the Prodigal Son, the thought is of man's seeking God. And seeking on both sides assuredly there must be, or there will be no finding; and then God and the soul, once apart, will stay apart. But the three illustrations picture forth one whole transaction—*the conversion of a sinful soul.* In the first two we see the outgoing of Divine mercy, in the third the responsive working of the human heart and conscience, issuing in repentance. The Saviour saves the sinner, and the sinner accepts salvation of the Saviour. The lost sheep would never have come back to the shepherd unless the shepherd had gone forth to find the sheep; and the father would have waited vainly at his door, unless the prodigal had made up his mind that he would arise and go to his father.

Now we ought not here to miss the lesson of the need there always is of looking all round a subject, and interpreting Scripture by Scripture. As our 20th Article of Religion has it, "neither may we so expound one place of Scripture that it be repugnant to another." That is the way of sectaries of every sort, fastening upon particular passages which seem, taken by themselves, to sustain some preconceived doctrine, and ignoring the rest, rather than interpreting one by another, and all by the analogy of the faith. For example, the Calvinist takes the first two of these parables, which set forth God's work in seeking and saving the soul, and interprets them as establishing his doctrine of sovereignty and *irresistible grace*—that He "hath mercy on whom He will have mercy, and whom He will He hardeneth." On the other hand, the Socinian finds in the voluntary return of the Prodigal Son evidence to establish his doctrine of the sufficiency of the human will and power, independently of Divine grace, to work out man's righteousness and consequent salvation. But the Church teaches that these two factors in the great

GOD'S SEEKING THE SINNER.

transaction are correlative and complementary. Positive statements, though they may be different, are often not contradictory. Negative statements are generally what keep men apart in their thinking. The relation of God and the soul is too large a matter to be comprised in one statement, or set forth by one illustration. Hence the twofold teaching of these three parables. God seeks the sinner and the sinner seeks God. And they find each other, because each wants to find and to be found of each.

In order to take in our Lord's teaching here, we must note who they were—two very different sets of people in some respects—that He was speaking to. "Then drew near unto Him all the publicans and sinners for to hear Him." That was one set of people. "And the Pharisees and scribes murmured, saying, This man receiveth sinners, and eateth with them." That was the other set of people. Each of these classes was well marked off, in the estimation of the other, and indeed in their own estimation. But it has been well said that if we would have influence with people we must not begin by classifying them, but by endeavoring to understand them. "The publicans and sinners drew near unto Him." No wonder, for they had never heard the like before to that which now they heard from Him. They had been classified enough, God knows; but here was One Who endeavored to understand them, and evidently did understand them. And the others found out that He understood them too. For deep down in the consciousness at least of some of these Pharisees must have been the conviction that, as they were the appointed shepherds of Israel, this new and (as they thought) self-appointed Shepherd was doing the very thing which they had left undone. "This man receiveth sinners," they complained. How very human it is to find fault with and criticise others for doing what we are conscious of neglecting! Without taking this occasion to rebuke their unfaithfulness, He gently plants a seed of wholesome reflection in their minds, and says, as it were, And why should I not? As a Shepherd sent from God—why should I not receive sinners? For what else am I come? It is the natural thing for Me to do. Why, "what man of you is there, having a hundred sheep, if he lose one of them, doth not leave the ninety and nine"—not in the desolate and dangerous desert indeed, but amid the green pastures and beside the still waters of the uncultivated commons where they are safely and quietly feeding—"and go after that which is lost, until he find it?" These parables were a gracious effort to get below the crust of Pharisaism to the underlying human nature, and to vindicate God's attribute of mercy. And to publicans and sinners of that and every age they are the very Gospel. For assuredly the Pharisee was not all Pharisee, nor the publican all sinner. What a patient teacher Jesus was! What a faithful, self-unsparing Shepherd then and now!

Taking then, first of all—for it comes first in order—*God's seeking the sinner*, let us note to-day the points which illustrate this in all three parables.

I. And first, they all set forth, most strikingly, *God's care for individual souls.*

There were a hundred sheep, and one only was in danger. But because it was in danger, the shepherd left the ninety and nine, and for the time being concentrated his care upon that one. The woman, too, almost forgot the nine pieces of silver, and searched diligently for the piece which was lost. The father took for granted that the son who was ever with him would stay there, and his longing was for the one who had gone away. They valued the lost, not for its intrinsic value, nor for its market value, but with that added appraisement of anxieties, fears, hopes, affections which we all add to our precious things when they are in peril—the appraisement of the heart.

Now it is very wonderful that on the throne of His mighty empire God should be touched by this natural human feeling, and regard the loss of an individual soul. But He is a Shepherd Who "calleth His own sheep by name." Not a star can fall from the firmament, nor a hair from our heads without His knowledge, and in His heart He holds and identifies and sympathizes in every one, and one by one. For does any one suppose that He regards bigness and overlooks littleness? Does He look only through the telescope of His knowledge, and not also through the microscope? And what average between the field of the microscope and the field of the telescope will you establish as the point at which things become worth His while? But bigness and littleness are not the standard of the heart, either human or Divine. Relationship is the standard, and we are related to Him. Every one of us *is His*. And He misses us, every one. "He sent His Son to seek and to save them that were lost."

II. And now, how shall we describe and define this loss? The loss, to God and to the soul, is in *the soul's getting apart from God*. And that which sets the soul off from conscious relation to God, whatever it be in form and expression, in its essence *that is sin*. Sin is not primarily *doing* wrong, it is *being* wrong—not so much an act as a condition.

See then how souls get lost, as illustrated in these three parables.

1. The sheep got lost through ignorance, silliness, stupidity. It was not so much to blame, and yet its gregarious instinct should have kept it with the flock, and its instinct of affection for its shepherd should have kept it near him, and the shepherd's training should have gone for something. Yet it was but a silly sheep after all, and

GOD'S SEEKING THE SINNER.

you cannot judge a sheep for its ignorance. But, all the same, its ignorance and silliness was a peril and a loss.

When people sin through ignorance and silliness they cannot be said to be responsible. They may be dimly conscious of something wrong, they know not exactly what ; may feel, somehow, that they are in the wrong place, they know not exactly where, or how they got there. They have gone against something within them, but the untutored conscience cannot define the fault. Somebody must go out after them, and not scold them for their wandering, nor drive them back with hard words, but carry them a bit, and show them where they belong. They are subjects, not for a penitentiary, but for a Rescue Mission wise and true. "We have erred and strayed from Thy ways like lost sheep."

2. It suits my purpose in passing on to the next parable, to depart from the strict letter of critical exegesis, though not, I trust, from the spirit of the Saviour's teaching. It has exercised commentators to know just how to explain the woman and her lost piece of money. I shall make a two-fold application of the parable by way of illustration.

The woman may stand for the Church. To her has been entrusted the care of human souls more precious than silver, and stamped with the image and superscription of the King—for "God made man in His own image." She is responsible for their care, and at fault when she loses them by neglect of anything she can do. This consciousness comes out in the expressions of the parables, for while the shepherd did not lose the sheep by any fault of his, and so when he finds it he says, "I have found *my sheep which was lost,*" the woman did lose the coin by her own fault, and so when she finds it she says, "I have found *the piece which I had lost.*" And when we say the Church is responsible for precious souls, what can we mean but this—that the ministers and the members of the Church are responsible? And what is it measures their responsibility but this—their abilities and their opportunities for teaching, training, guiding, helping human souls into the better life? I could wish that at all times, and especially just now when we are re-organizing our Sunday-school work, the members of the Church, and particularly the women of the Church, who are the natural keepers of young souls, could realize this responsibility. It is so easy to merge the sense of individual duty in the general parochial duty, and to think the rector will find somebody to do it, when the rector is at his wit's end to know what to do with the children who come, and is tempted to wish that no more would come, when he ought to be going out after them, and sweeping diligently till he finds them. We baptize from fifty to seventy children every year—signing the cross upon their brows to mark them with the King's seal—and where are they? Not in the Sunday-school, for want of able and faithful teachers—lost *in the house*, within the very Church itself. The candle which the woman lighted is the word of God—*that* finds children's minds and hearts amid the dust of worldliness—but somebody must sweep diligently, notwithstanding it is so much easier to let the dust lie, and the coin lie buried in it. This is one application of the parable.

But to make a more personal application: The woman may represent our very selves, considered as keepers of our own souls. To each of us God has entrusted our own immortal spirits, made in His image and sealed as His. For indeed we are in a very true sense responsible for the keeping of ourselves, and the Saviour in another place asks, "What shall it profit a man if he gain the whole world, and lose his own soul?"

Now there is this difference in the two parables, that in the first, the sheep, being endowed with power of motion, is lost by act of its own —it goes away into the wilderness. But the piece of money, being inert matter, falls by its own weight when the hand is loosed that held it. It takes no action in getting lost, but is simply passive. Here a new thought is introduced, a new principle and spiritual fact comes into view. The principle is that of inherent tendency downward, the law of gravitation to evil which is so evidently a fact and a factor in our spiritual character and experience. Explain it how we will, somebody must keep hold of us lest we fall. We call this downward tendency original sin, and trace it to Adam; but however we account for it, and whatever we call it, the strenuous moral effort that is made in our behalf by the family under the impulsion of parental love, by the State in its care for self-preservation, and by the Church in love and duty to God, all goes to show that human nature cannot be left to itself, but must be held on to or it is lost. To the danger of spiritual loss from ignorant and stupid wandering, is added the peril of neglect. As the neglected garden runs to weeds, as the coin negligently handled falls into the dust, so the soul simply uncared for gets apart from God. This I take to be the special and peculiar illustration of this second parable.

3. The third parable, however, brings us face to face with the most serious of all spiritual possibilities, the getting apart from God which comes of *wilful sin*—the deliberate choice of evil, the deliberate rejection of God. Calmly, and of set purpose, the prodigal son gathers together what he can lay claim to, and more than he can rightly claim, and leaves his father's house. This parable, in this point, needs no explanation. "We have erred and strayed from Thy ways like lost sheep." "There is no health in us." But more

than this, "we have done," and done wilfully, "those things which we ought not to have done, and left undone those things which we ought to have done." Three sorts of sin. Three ways of getting apart from God. And the last the worst.

III. Now look at the ways of recovery. Ways, did I say? There is but one way—"I am the Way," saith Christ.

1. "I am the Good Shepherd," saith He again, for many illustrations do but set forth the one Saviour.

He did not declare His Divinity to the Pharisees. The times were not ripe, and their minds were not ripe for that—not that they could not, but that they would not take it in. He was content to have them recognize Him, if they would, simply as a Shepherd, having a mission to the lost sheep of the house of Israel, doing what they neither did nor yet desired to do, and indicating the compassionate ways of God. But to the publicans and sinners who came to Him there must have been that in His gracious personality, in the inner knowledge He showed of their needs and their capacities, in the deep love for their souls that spoke in His voice and looked forth from His eye, which revealed Him to them as something more than lawgiver and prophet had ever even claimed to be, One sent from God to find them and bring them back. They might not know who He was, but they knew *Him*, believed in Him, trusted Him, loved Him, followed Him.

Now it is this personal contact of the soul with Christ, as revealed in the Gospel—this looking into His eye, this touching of His hand, this very sounding of His voice in human ears, which comes with the open-hearted study of the Scriptures that make Him known to us—this is the means of spiritual conversion, of bringing us back to God who have gotten away from Him. It was necessary that the Good Shepherd should go out after the lost sheep until He find it. For, though in silliness and ignorance the sheep may wander from the fold, they are little likely to wander back to it without the Shepherd's seeking. Any way will lead out and away from the fold, but only one way leads back into it, and the chances are against their happening to take that way. The wandering may be aimless, but the return must be aimful, purposeful. From centre to circumference we may go on any line, straight or crooked, but from circumference to centre only on one—the fold is just a point in the great wilderness. And so the sheep would never have come back if the Shepherd had not gone out after it and found it. This is the teaching of the first parable as to the way of recovery.

2. The teaching of the second is to the same point. The woman lit her candle, and swept the house diligently till she found the piece of

money that had slipped away from her hand. The Church is God's care-taker of His precious ones. When she awakes to the fact that she has lost one of them in the dust of earth—lost it, aye, in the very house which is called, as being hers, the Church (never mind the mixing of the figure), she sweeps the house; she disturbs the quiet of those of her members who do not like to be disturbed with clouds of dust, and think things are well enough as they are; she moves settled things about, and sweeps diligently till she finds it. This she does if she is true to her duty as a Church. She preaches, she teaches, she has missions, she holds up her candle aflame with the word of God to sinners; she leaves no dusty corners for old abuses and neglects; the burden of lost souls is heavy upon her. For she is set in the world to carry on Christ's personal work of recovery. And woe to the Church, and to the ministers and members of the Church, each in his several sphere, and according to his several ability, if they are content that souls should slip from their care—their own souls or others— and they not seek diligently until they find them. This is the teaching of this second parable. Both together they set forth the *seeking love of God*.

3. It might seem at first as if in the parable of the Prodigal Son there was no suggestion of God's seeking, but only of the sinner's voluntary return. I think, however, we should miss

some of the tenderness and beauty of this matchless story if we failed to take in the thought of the abiding power of known and trusted love to draw back the heart of the wanderer. For what do you think, after all, was the prodigal's inducement to return? Was it altogether the failure and wreck of his present, the homelessness, the friendlessness, the want, the bitter taste of spent pleasures? Or was it *that*, in contrast with the warmth, the love of home? Happy is he who, in his wanderings away from God, retains the memory of a Christian home, of a Christian father's and mother's love and teaching; of the Church in which he was baptized, and, it may be, confirmed; of the Bible out of which he learned his daily text; and, more than all, who can recall his early conceptions of God as his Heavenly Father; of the moving story of his Saviour's Birth and Passion; who still has old ideas of spiritual grace and help, and dwells regretfully upon the memory of innocent years in which he did not fear to lift his childish eyes and look into the face of God. He yet may come to feel, and not resist it, the drawing power of love.

Thus these three parables all set forth one part of this great transaction of the soul's return to God—*God's seeking of the sinner.* Another day we will consider the correlative and complementary part, the sinner's seeking of God. For in this wonderful trilogy of Scripture teaching is contained the Gospel of deliverance for sinful souls.

THE SINNER'S SEEKING GOD.

S. JOHN'S, STAMFORD, FEBRUARY 11, 1894.

THE SINNER'S SEEKING GOD.

"He arose, and came to his father."—St. Luke xv. 20.

A man is never less his own master than when he undertakes to be his own master: *i.e.,* to live without law. And, on the other hand, that is true which the Prayer Book says, "God's service is perfect freedom."

This, which may be observed any day among living men, is illustrated in the story of the Prodigal Son's determined effort to do as he liked. He only succeeded in making a change of masters, and that for the worse. A man begins sometimes by resenting the fact that he cannot do the evil that he would, and ends by discovering with dismay that he cannot do the good that he would. It is terrible when the interference with freedom comes from below.

Not long since we considered the three parables in the 15th chapter of St. Luke, which set forth the coming together of God and the soul, after they have been put apart by sin. The parables of the Lost Sheep and the Lost Piece of Money illustrate God's seeking man. The parable of the Prodigal Son illustrates man's seeking God, and this we take up to-day.

The erring and straying of the lost sheep stands for sins of ignorance and infirmity. The loss of the coin sets forth the natural gravitation of the soul to evil. But the sin of the Prodigal was wilful sin, and the worst. The salvation of the first was by some one going out after it. The salvation of the second was by some one holding on to it. The salvation of the third was by his own coming back. But it must be remembered that these three representations do not set forth different classes of sins and sinners, but different aspects of the spiritual situation of all sinners. We are all lost sheep and need bringing back, We all have tendencies to evil, and need to be held on to. We are all disobedient children, and must make up our own minds to come back. The Saviour, the Church, and our own wills have each and all their parts in our personal salvation. In distinction from the first two parables, the third sets forth the change of heart which is involved in a true conversion.

For a man has a will of his own and nobody can convert him. Alone among created things, he can stand out against his God. Sin of ignorance cannot ruin him. Original sin cannot ruin him. But wilful sin—the deliberate choice of evil—can, and will.

The Prodigal Son made deliberate choice of evil. How graphically this is told! He was the son of an affluent and honorable family of the house of Israel. From infancy he had been a member of the Church. He had been educated in the knowledge of God and duty. He was not ignorant. He had been the recipient of God's grace—that inward and spiritual force which is given to us all to counteract the downward tendency of original sin. Helps to right feeling and right living were around him and within him. He grew up, as we should say, in the atmosphere of a Christian home. He could not put the blame on heredity or on circumstances. It was on himself, and he knew it.

How deliberate he was! He knew what he was about, though he did not realize all the consequences. For years he had been growing restive under the restraints of Church and home. His will and choices had been growing more and more out of harmony with the will of his father and with his God. More and more he resented his restricted liberty. He wanted freedom to exercise what he called his discretion, to manage his own affairs; in short, to do as he liked. And so at length he determined to bring on the issue, "Father, give me the portion of goods that falleth to me." He claimed his separate interest. Sin is unsocial, selfish, impatient of common interests, and common responsibilities, and common joys and privileges. His father's family was to him a nuisance—the Church still more so. Love had died out, for love is social. He began to hate his father, and his God, because they were a restraint upon him.

And so, when it came to that, and his father saw it had come to that, the father knew then that home was home no longer, and with heavy heart "he divided unto him his living," and let him go. The son lingered a few days longer—with what thoughts and feelings we can well imagine, for it was a tremendous step to take, when he began to realize it, and the stimulus of opposition was withdrawn, and the memories of kindness came back, and all the good in him was stirred. But he "gathered all together," and went at last.

Pass over now the details of his downward course, and see him again at the bottom of it, and note the processes of his recovery. For our story is the story of a soul's return to God.

What brought him back? For, *he came back*, and of his own accord. That is, he acted on motives.

First of all, in the order of motives, as is evident, was *his misery*. Passing over the details of the story, and the still more pathetic detail of a soul's suffering which these represent, we note *the misery of disappointment.*

He went away in pursuit of happiness. But happiness consists in the fitness and harmony of our surroundings with our very selves.

Little did this gentleman born, accustomed not merely to the comforts, but to the refinements of life, and especially to that moral refinement which we call the tone of *really* good society—little did he conceive of the sordidness he was to encounter in that "far country" for which he set out so expectantly. Its citizens, he found, were not of the sort he had been used to. It was impossible he should have taken this in when he started. But when his money was gone, which kept him within the range of that imitation quality which answers for a time for the real quality, which is moral, and not material, and he got amid the dregs of society, he felt the contrast. It was husks for bread. It was tyranny instead of law, the company of swine-herds for the society of the home.

It is one, and not the least, of the losses that befall one who sinks below the level of the high and pure life of the Christian home and Church in which he was born and bred, especially when he sinks into the sensual life of vice and sin, that he loses self-respect and respect for his surroundings. For the Christian life, however humble the social environment, however uncultured, and poor, and plain, is, after all, a life passed among elevating thoughts and things. A Christian, in so far as he is a Christian, is never vulgar. The best and highest in him is brought out. Religion has affinity for whatever is elevated and elevating in the plainest and humblest man. In conventional manners he may be lacking, but in the manners that "maketh man" he

THE SINNER'S SEEKING GOD.

is not lacking, because unselfishness is the essential characteristic of the true nobleman, and it is also the true outcome of religion. It was the lower part in this well-bred prodigal that spoke out and said, "Give me the portion of goods that falleth to me"; but when he got among the sordidnesses of the lower life, then the higher and better part in him remembered the higher sort of life in which he had been bred, and the contrast was a bitter one to him in his better moments. I remember a college man of brilliant parts, who had sunk into the dregs, telling me that when he was standing in the crowd at the funeral of President Lincoln, he saw his brother, a clergyman, and felt an unutterable longing to speak to him; but the recollections of their early home so rushed in upon him and overwhelmed him with the shame of his degradation that he could not do it. The bitterest recollection that comes, I doubt not, to many a man in the lowest depths, is not of the comforts he has lost, but of the morally high things, the atmosphere of purity, from which he has fallen. For sin is degrading, and even though it be still chosen, it is despised, and the sinner who follows his lower lusts is self-despised, as well as self-condemned. The loss of self-respect is the keenest misery.

I wish my voice could reach the ear of some young men of Christian families, and impress them with a sense of the degradation of that slavery to sensual lusts to which they will some

THE SINNER'S SEEKING GOD.

day awaken, if the better part in them do not become brutalized. For "the saddest of all sad words" are these, "It might have been." The misery of disappointment!

But the better part in this prodigal did *not* become utterly brutalized. His better self spoke out at last, and his better self was, after all, *himself*. It was when he came to himself that he said, "I will arise and go to my father."

We are often disappointed in the results of Christian home training and Church training. We cannot see why it is that young men of Christian families, whose parents are earnest and consistent Christian people, respected in the community, careful in bringing up their children, and setting a good example to them, why the sons of such families should go astray. They often do, however, and there is no explanation to be given of it, so far as we can see. If there have been, after all, defects in the family training—too much severity, or too little, unevenness of temper, a self-indulgent way of living, a worldly standard—all these may be detected by the clear-eyed boy at home though they may escape the outside ken. And these things weaken the Christian influence of the home which we all thought so pure and strong. But after all the fact remains that children go astray when least expected to do so.

Of this, however, be sure, that they carry with them recollections, influences, principles, moral and spiritual perceptions, that tend to bring them back. They are not easy and satisfied in evil living. *They know the difference.* The more violent and demonstrative they are in sin, and in the unbelief which sin produces, often, the more they feel themselves in the wrong. The standard remains imbedded in their consciousness—their bringing up is a part of them. And, sometimes through God's providences, and sometimes out of very weariness and disappointment, but always with the help of God's grace, the soul looks homeward with longing for the well-remembered bread in the father's house—the food on which it was nurtured, and which it craves again. If any of you have prodigal sons, do not give up hope, and do not give up prayer.

And now let us see what we can learn, from the story, *of the manner of the soul's seeking God.*

He made up his mind to return. It was an act of will. The going out was *wilful.* The return was *willing.* He was not *brought back* like the wandering sheep—that is not the aspect in which the conversion is presented here, though it is one aspect of conversion. Here is implied the sinner's free agency in the return to God. "I will arise and go." "And he arose and came."

Here was, to begin with, an *act of faith.* He believed in his father. He believed in his father's love and forgivingness. He knew his father well enough to believe in that. He was deterred by

THE SINNER'S SEEKING GOD.

no fear that the father might have chosen and elected the elder son, and reprobated him. He had no anxiety as to his welcome.

What a mercy it is when God's prodigals are not restrained from trusting Him by early training in false and grim theologies—gospels of despair. Thank God that in the Church Catechism which your children are taught there is nothing about election and reprobation; that it begins by telling them that they are "members of Christ, children of God, and inheritors of the kingdom of heaven," and goes on from that. They will never forget those words of the Catechism—the very foundation of practical theology. They will always know where God stands towards them. The conception of God which a child gets in our Sunday-school makes despair impossible, and hope always possible. His baptism is the seal of his sonship. He, his very self, is the child of God; and when he comes to himself he says, "I will arise and go to my Father." There are just such home-comings every day.

Then, again, this prodigal made up his mind to confess. "I will say unto him, Father, I have sinned." He did not say he had made a mistake. He did not stop even with the confession that he had made a fool of himself. He said, "Father, I have sinned against heaven and before thee, and am no more worthy to be called thy son." He came back, himself again, leaving all his evil behind him.

It is instructive to note, just here, the reserve of a still proud spirit. He made up his mind to ask, on coming home, for the position of a servant—not of a son, for of that he was not worthy. He was ready to take his punishment—the loss of his proper station. He wanted to make amends by service, and not to claim position and property which he had had, and squandered. I think we can understand him. This attitude of his has its parallel in the reluctance of the sinner to throw himself utterly on the mercy of God. We would rather not be under obligations, if it were possible, even to our Maker. At any rate, let us reduce them. We would all like to earn forgiveness, somehow, to make amends, to save some little remnant of what we call our independence and self-respect. When once we get into the Father's presence, however, we find and feel ourselves on very different ground from that. No making up for the past, no thought of restitution, is possible in the soul's true relation to God. Obligations!—that is, mercies—we accept them lovingly, because they are born of love. We receive them ungrudgingly, even as they are given.

For, look now at the welcome he got. The father had been forgiving him—was in an attitude for forgivingness all the time. The alienation had not been on his part. The picture which the parable presents to us is of the father going to the door to look out, and see if perchance the wanderer might be coming back. Often and often he had done that, when one morning he sees an approaching figure—yes, yes, it *is* he—and "he ran, and fell on his neck, and kissed him."

Surely this representation of the Heavenly Father's attitude toward the sinner should make repentance easier ! Take it into your minds and hearts, ye who have wandered from Him into ways of sin, and know ye that He is more anxious for you than you are for yourselves. Know that He never forgets His children—never says, "My son has made his bed, let him lie on it." His Fatherhood is infinite.

And see how that brings out the sonliness. That speech of his about coming back into the house as a servant, which the high-spirited lad had prepared when he was in the far country, and which seemed to him then so exactly the thing to say—*he never said it.* He could not say it, it seemed so foreign to the actual situation. The idea, with his head on his father's shoulder, to talk about coming back as a hired servant ! To earn his living rather than to accept it !

Ah ! if we can only get our souls into God's very presence, where "perfect love casteth out fear," casteth out pride, casteth out self, and the tired heart resteth in the bosom of infinite and eternal love !

ST. BARNABAS THE APOSTLE.

ST. BARNABAS' DAY, S. JOHN'S, STAMFORD, JUNE 11, 1882.

ST. BARNABAS THE APOSTLE.

"He was a good man, and full of the Holy Ghost and of faith: and much people was added unto the Lord."—ACTS xi. 24.

This is the description which Scripture gives of the character of Barnabas the Apostle, and of the results of his work. He is one of the minor characters of the New Testament history, not commanding our attention and admiration, as St. Peter and St. Paul, by his great personality or by the magnitude of his Apostolic work. But none the less on that account is he a quiet study for the people who, like ourselves, are neither great nor admirable; but who yet would like to have it said of us also, "a good man, full of the Holy Ghost and of faith," and of the results of our homely, useful life and example, "much people was added to the Lord."

He is none the worse for our purpose because he had a fault or two, if he was a saint. None of us could be as great as Paul if we tried. But I think, if we tried, some of us might be as good as Barnabas, and as useful in a modest way. The course of the Christian year has brought us face to face with very high themes of late: the Ascension of our Lord, His Commission to the Church, the Office of the Holy Ghost, the Divinity of Christ. We are not sorry to have our strained attention turned to-day to the humbler study of the life-lessons in the history of a Christian man.

His proper name, we read, was Joses, and he was probably one of those foreign Jews who on the day of Pentecost were "dwelling at Jerusalem, devout men, out of every nation under heaven." The Jews were then, as ever since, largely the merchants and bankers of the world, and around the eastern end of the Mediterranean the world's business was chiefly carried on. His residence was in the island of Cyprus, and he was a man of property. Moreover, being of the tribe of Levi, he was likely to be well versed in Hebrew literature; and in the contact of religious truth with the actual life of men outside of religious circles, there had come to him that influence of humanity upon theology which is an important element of success in a religious teacher. If a preacher has no theology he will never elevate men; if he has no humanity he will never even influence them.

1. The first quality of character which we note in him is the mingled tact and tenderness which his fellow-Apostles, who knew him best, must have recognized in him when they surnamed him "Barnabas," which is, being interpreted, "The Son of Consolation." I am aware that the recent revisers of the New Testament, with that singular facility which in so many instances they

ST. BARNABAS THE APOSTLE.

have manifested for turning poetry into prose, have translated his name into "The Son of Exhortation." I do not believe that inspired Apostles were ever guilty of anything so inane as to compliment one another with the title of a good exhorter. They were all exhorters, no doubt; but I should hope they were something more, and prefer to believe that among the "singular gifts" with which God endued His holy Apostle Barnabas, was the rare gift of consolation. Exhortation is cheap; consolation, the power of comforting, is precious. And the word which in our old Bibles is translated "consolation," is the same word which St. Paul uses unmistakably in this sense in that sweet passage in II. Cor. i. 3, 4: "Blessed be God, . . . the God of all comfort; Who comforteth us in all our tribulation, that we may be able to comfort them which are in any trouble, by the comfort wherewith we ourselves are comforted of God." One could almost think St. Paul had his friend and companion Barnabas in mind when he thought about comforting, and recalled some special instances of the comfort he himself had received in the manifold and troubled experiences of missionary life which he passed through in the restful and healing companionship of "The Son of Consolation."

We know, at all events, of one such instance. It is the occasion referred to in the 9th chapter of the Acts, when Saul, after his conversion, was come to Jerusalem, and "assayed to join himself to the disciples ; but they were all afraid of him, and believed not that he was a disciple." It was a hard spot for the enthusiastic young convert to find himself in. The opposition of the enemies of Christ only roused and stimulated, but the suspicion of brethren in the faith chilled and disheartened him. It was at this juncture that Barnabas, with tact and tenderness, and the ready sympathy of a humane and gentle soul, took him by the hand and brought him to the Apostles, and vouched for the reality of the change that had come over Saul the persecutor, and stood sponsor for the new made Christian. It required some moral courage, too—and courage is always necessary in a consoler—some courage to face the prejudices of the companions and friends of Stephen, and ask them to take his murderer into their hearts and receive him as one of themselves. But it is an essential part of the office of the consoler to rectify wrong and troublous situations which one naturally shrinks from tackling, and to undertake which involves the assumption of delicate and difficult responsibilities, of interference in the affairs of others which none but a brave soul will willingly assume. It is far easier to do what most of us are often doing—leave people to get out of hard spots as best they may, so they do not trouble us as we pass by on the other side. Tact, to know what to do and how to do it; tenderness, to sympathize in

ST. BARNABAS THE APOSTLE.

situations and be impelled to rectify them; courage, to be willing to face their difficulties; these are singular gifts of the Holy Ghost, developing natural elements of character, and forming some of us even in our day, into sons of consolation, to alleviate, if only just a little, the sorrows of mankind.

And, thinking of the Church, as we ought to think of it, as the rounded and completed Body of Christ, in which each part is the complement of every other, so that if one member suffer, all the members suffer with it, it is pleasant and instructive to remember that there was a "Son of Consolation" among the first Apostles and founders of the Church. Let us try to perpetuate this Apostolic succession, and pray God, as in the Collect for St. Barnabas' Day, that He will not leave His Church destitute of this among His "manifold gifts," nor suffer us to fail of grace to "use it alway to His honor and glory." For, this "miserable and naughty world" will always have use for sons of consolation.

2. The second element which we note in the character of Barnabas is *his generosity*. He was a large-minded and large-hearted man.

To begin with, he was generous with his property. And that is the first and most obvious thing for a man to be generous with; and if he cannot find in his heart to be generous with that, be sure he is not generous at all. The first thing we read about Barnabas is that, "having land, he sold it, and brought the money, and laid it at the Apostles' feet."

He evidently belonged to a wealthy family. It was his sister, Mary, who opened her ample house to the Christians in Jerusalem at the time of Herod's persecution, where many were gathered together praying, after the beheading of James the Apostle, and the imprisonment of St. Peter. She evidently had some of her brother's qualities, and while she retained control of her property, she used it as he, in another way, had used his, for the benefit of the Church and the succor of the Lord's people. She had a family, the evangelist, St. Mark, was her son, and therefore she provided first for her own house. But her brother was unmarried, as St. Paul intimates when he connects Barnabas with himself as having the same right to marry that Peter and the other Apostles had, implying that he and Barnabas had not exercised the right. (I. Cor. ix. 6.) And therefore his property had no claims upon it, his relatives having enough of their own, and he was at liberty to use it for the public good, and did so. He gave it to the Church.

In this he is the example of those who, in every age, have been conspicuous for large benefactions to the cause of humanity and religion. He did not calculate how little he could get off with in the matter of giving. He did not trouble himself about what others gave or did not give, nor limit himself to what he considered "his share" of the Church expenses. He felt that when he gave for Church purposes he was giving to God, and not to man. There was a man, soon after—we find the story in the very next chapter—who, with his wife, gave because others gave, gave "grudgingly and of necessity," and whose meanness comes into contiguity and contrast with the generosity of Barnabas, and whose end was different. Now let me say here that such benefactions as that of Barnabas are to be expected in the Christian Church. You find them in all the ages of Christianity—the large endowments for charity, the institutions, the magnificent churches which lift the externals of religion above sordidness, these have not been created out of the measured offerings of people willing to do "their share"— no less, indeed, than their share, but assuredly no more. There have been, and there are Christians, who do not stint, who desire to do what they *can*, and not what they *must;* if there were not, the world would be worse off than it is, and so should we. The example of Barnabas may teach those who have property to be generous in their contribution of it for the public good. But then, he had given himself, you know, and the rest followed.

No wonder, that when the rich Gentile Christians of Antioch wanted to send a contribution of their worldly things for the relief of the poor and famine-stricken Christians at Jerusalem, through whom they had received so largely in spiritual things, and wanted to be sure that it would be liberally and with tact and tenderness dispensed, they chose as their messenger and almoner the generous Son of Consolation.

This, however, was not the only way in which the generosity of Barnabas appeared. He was a large-minded and large-hearted man, and this appears in other ways than simply giving money. For large legacies have been left to the Church, sometimes, by very curious people.

There is an incident—two incidents, rather—recorded in the 11th chapter of the Acts, which afford a little character-study. Antioch, in Syria, was a wealthy and influential community—St. Peter seems to have become afterward the Bishop of it (not of Rome)—and through the preaching of some of those who were exiled from Jerusalem, in the persecution in which Stephen lost his life (in part through the agency of Saul), many of the Jews and Gentiles of that city received the Gospel. Now, it was very hard, as we know, for the Jerusalem Christians to take in the idea of Gentiles being brought into the Church, and so they cast about for some one to go to Antioch and look into the case. They pitched upon Barnabas, as being Jewish enough in his feelings to be trusted in that particular, and yet, as having lived in Cyprus, where it seems these enterprising preachers came from, calculated to deal with the matter in that particular, also. Now, one element of a generous character is fair-mindedness, and so we find that when Barnabas got to Antioch, and saw unmistakable evidence that the grace of God was in the work going on there, his Jewish prejudices gave way, and he "was glad" to see the progress of the truth, and helped the good cause with his own approving and sympathetic words, "and exhorted them all that with purpose of heart they would cleave unto the Lord." And then follows the comment, in the words of our text to-day, "For he was a good man, and full of the Holy Ghost and of faith; and much people was added unto the Lord." "A good man"— what can this mean, in this connection, except that he was generous and unselfish enough to rise above his prejudices of race; that he loved truth and goodness wherever he saw it, and gave it welcome to his heart; that the Holy Ghost had given him faith enough in God and truth to feel that it was all right, even if people did not pronounce the Shibboleth, and that where God's spiritual power went, he was glad that it should go. We can hardly appreciate it, not being Jerusalem Jews turned Christians, and yet I think there are some Churchmen who might learn the lesson. It was that way of dealing with the subject that produced the result spoken of, "and much people was added unto the Lord."

But here follows another illustration of his

generosity of soul: "Then departed Barnabas to Tarsus, for to seek Saul. And when he had found him, he brought him to Antioch." Why should he go for Saul? Because, setting himself and his own priority of rank and position aside, he recognizes the pre-eminent ability and fitness of the new and as yet untried Apostle of the Gentiles, and his right, as such, to take the leading part in the mission. He is intent on one thing, *the conversion of men to Christ,* and wants always the best thing to be done to promote it. Henceforth he takes a secondary position in missionary work, and is known in subsequent history as the companion of St. Paul. It takes a large man to accept gracefully and to work faithfully and self-forgetfully in a small position.

The story of his companionship with St. Paul in labors, in perils, in sufferings, and in successes, need not be told. He was no unworthy co-worker with the great Apostle, and though he kept himself in the background he was not always placed there by others. The people of Lystra when they were possessed with the idea that the two Apostles were gods come down in the likeness of men, took Barnabas, with his dignity and benignity, for Jupiter, father of gods and men; and Paul, eager, active, and of less majestic mien, for the messenger-god Mercurius.

The friendship, no doubt, lasted their lifetime, but the intimacy and co-working terminated in a sharp dissension as to details, which reveals the human nature in both.

I said he had a fault or two. Fortunately, for perfect saints are not of much use to us poor sinners in the way of example. And, as is often found to be the case, his faults were the outgrowth of his virtues. His sympathetic nature led him into a weakness.

He was intimate with St. Paul for eleven years, but it took longer than that to get the Judaizing tendency out of him. He sympathized with the situation and views of the Gentile Christians when he was with them, and sympathized with the traditional views and feelings of the Jewish Christians when he was with them. He was not so strong a man, clear-headed and logical, as St. Paul, who never swerved in his grasp of a principle, or shrank from carrying it to its practical conclusions, out of tenderness for either friends or foes. He alone, Apostle of the Gentiles, consistently maintained the absolute equality, in the Christian Church, of those who had been circumcised members of the Jewish Church, and the uncircumcised Gentiles ; and, while not needlessly offending Jewish sentiment, he refused to bind Gentile Christians with the yoke of the Jewish ceremonial law. The conflict of new principles with old habits is apparent in the conduct of all other Apostles, and I cannot help thinking, reverently, that it was this lingering adhesion to the past on their part that brought it about that they were not used by the Holy Spirit, as St. Paul was, to frame epistles which should be standards of doctrine and practice for the future ages of mankind. St. Paul's epistle to the Galatians bears evidence of the conflict of opinion going on in the early Church; it is a passionate argument and appeal for the broader principles of Christianity as against the narrower traditions of Judaism. And in it he speaks of his contest in this interest with St. Peter and other Jews when, on the occasion I have before referred to, they came to Antioch, and then adds, that "Barnabas also was carried away with their dissimulation."

This latent difference in their way of looking at things was at the bottom of their disagreement. But they might have worked together, notwithstanding, except for a circumstance which occurred in connection with Mark, the nephew of Barnabas, to whom he was evidently much attached. The young man started with them on their first missionary journey, but quitted them before they had gone very far. There seems to be reason for thinking that he gave up the work among the Gentiles because he was still so largely under the influences of Jewish prejudices that he could not thoroughly sympathize with St. Paul. There was strong personal attachment, as well as doctrinal sympathy, between him and St. Peter, who speaks of him as "Marcus, my son." And therefore when the time came for the second missionary journey of Paul and Barnabas, and the latter proposed to take his nephew with them again, Paul objected —he was "not willing to take him with them who departed from them in Pamphylia, and went not with them to the work." Some progress in ideas there had been since then, for the Council of Jerusalem had formally settled some of the vexed questions of the time, but still some of the Jewish Christians had been convinced against their will, and the earnest and thorough-going Paul felt that he could not thoroughly trust them in the missionary work. And so a personal element entered into the discussion, and "the contention was so sharp between them" that they separated, and Paul took Titus with him (a young Greek who had never been a Jew at all), and went one way, and Barnabas took Mark and went to work in his native island of Cyprus.

And so we see there was some human nature in Apostles after all; if there had not been, they would never have converted the world, for the world was earthly, and the heavenly treasure had to be offered to it in earthen vessels. So is the wisdom of God to-day, and we learn from the faults of Apostles—and their successors—that the excellency of the power is of God, and not of us.

None the less, but all the more may we all learn lessons to-day from the life of this sweet-natured, considerate, kindly gentleman, whom God endued with singular gifts of the Holy Ghost. And in like manner we may pray for ourselves, as in the collect for St. Barnabas' Day, "Leave us not, we beseech Thee, destitute of Thy manifold gifts, nor yet of grace to use them," as he did, "alway to Thy honor and glory."

WORLDLY POLICY.

S. JOHN'S, STAMFORD, 1882.

WORLDLY POLICY.

"And Amaziah said to the man of God, But what shall we do for the hundred talents?"—II. CHRON. xxv. 9.

This chapter narrates the history of Amaziah's reign of twenty-nine years over the kingdom of Judah. The story is brief, but it is an instance of that felicity of description which characterizes the Scripture narratives—a single incident, delineated in a few strong, sharp lines, setting before us the character of the man.

Intent upon a war with the Edomites, the young king mustered his troops, and found them "300,000 choice men, able to go forth to war." Not content with this formidable force, however, "he hired also 100,000 mighty men of valour out of Israel for an hundred talents of silver." We shall better understand the error and the sin of the king of Judah when we remember the character and position, at this time, of the neighboring kingdom of Israel. It comprised the ten tribes which had seceded from the ancient united Hebrew kingdom, and had forsaken also the true God. They were idolaters, and their king was Joash, who "did evil in the sight of the Lord." This mass of idolatrous leaven Amaziah was willing to introduce into his kingdom and his army rather than lean only on the arm of the

God of battles. "But there came a man of God to him, saying, O king, let not the army of Israel go with thee, for the Lord is not with Israel." The remonstrance would seem to have been received ungraciously, for the prophet adds, "But if thou wilt go, do it, be strong for the battle: God shall make thee fall before the enemy, for God hath power to help and to cast down." The warning was in part successful; the king yielded to the main point. But there was a difficulty. "And Amaziah said to the man of God, But what shall we do for the hundred talents which I have given to the army of Israel? And the man of God answered, The Lord is able to give thee much more than this. Then Amaziah separated them, to wit, the army that was come to him out of Ephraim, to go home again: wherefore their anger was greatly kindled against Judah, and they returned home in great anger."

Such is the brief but vivid sketch which Scripture gives of this incident in Amaziah's life. He had done wrong. He was admonished that his wrong-doing would not prosper, and so he retraced his steps. But he did it reluctantly. He had religion enough to feel the force of the prophet's words: "God hath power to help and to cast down," but not enough to silence all objections, and determine him on doing the will of God, be the consequences what they may. He decides, on the whole, to let his doubtful allies go; but his querulous enquiry, half of distrust and half of covetous regret for his money thrown away, is, "But what shall we do for the hundred talents?" Is it absolutely necessary that the men should go? Can we not make some compromise by which I shall have my money's worth, without at the same time forfeiting the favor of God?

A very desirable arrangement, this would seem, to the Amaziahs in every age. For he is a representative character, and we shall be at no loss to trace among ourselves those principles of worldly policy which actuated him.

For, observe in the first place how worldly policy often hinders men from living and acting on true principles, and especially on Christian principles.

Take the instance of a man who has been brought up to respect religion, and who does respect it, and admits its claims upon him, but yet is not an avowedly Christian man. To him God's messenger comes and says: You are living without God in the world, and therefore you are living in vain. Have you laid your plans for wealth? "The blessing of God, it maketh rich," and "His are the silver and the gold"— how can you leave Him out of your plan of life? Are you pursuing happiness? You will fall short of it just in so far as you stop short of Him. "Seek first the Kingdom of God, and His righteousness, and all these things shall be added unto you." Such reasonings are unanswerable, and convince even when they fail to persuade. But the tempter suggests a difficulty: I do not see how I can make any radical change in my plan of life without serious disarrangement; I have invested so much of my time, and labor, and means; I am so committed to certain courses; I shall have to sacrifice so many advantages, and to adopt a system which, I greatly fear, will not succeed as the world is constituted. I wish the world were different, but as it is, I feel obliged to do things which my conscience does not altogether approve.

O trifler with solemn convictions! go on, if thou wilt. You have free will to evil; there is no compulsion to good. You can sear your conscience by perseverance in known sin. "If thou wilt go, do it; be strong—in your own strength—for the battle: God shall make thee fall before the enemy"; His eternal laws will vindicate themselves upon you; for "God hath power to help and to cast down."

Or perhaps a man may purpose, in a general way, to follow his conscience, and choose the service of God as the principle of his life, and yet not get entirely beyond the reach of the worldliness around, or above the worldliness within him. Worldly policy hampers men who are, in the main, endeavoring to lead Christian lives, and what is needed is a more hearty and uncompromising faith in God. For such as are tempted

WORLDLY POLICY.

to combine religion with worldliness, the history of Amaziah contains also a lesson. The key to his character is also the key to theirs, "He did that which was right in the sight of the Lord, *but not with a perfect heart.*" They have a general intention of doing the will of God, but their religious life is continually hampered by a worldly way of looking at things.

1. How often, for example, does worldly policy supersede religious principle in the management of business? The statement of high principles from the pulpit commends itself to the conscience of every man, and nobody would say of the Ten Commandments, as read out in church, that they do not apply. But conceive, if you can, the systematic statement and commendation, from the pulpit, of the maxims and principles which do actually govern many professedly Christian men in business matters. Let the preacher construct a system of business ethics *founded on fact,* and promulgate it here. He would be denounced as a betrayer of his trust; as one who loved to talk of lies more than righteousness; as undermining the foundations of public morality; as profaning the holy place and time. Men would say, "Thou lovest to speak all words that may do hurt, O thou false tongue." For, in this place, such a translation of actions into words would at once be tested by those principles of natural and revealed religion which every unperverted conscience recognizes

as the true principles of life. They would be seen in the white light of eternal Truth and eternal Right.

But, surely, this is the light in which a man should wish always to view the principles he is living on. If they will not bear it, they had better be abandoned now. If they are not fit to be stated in church, they are not fit to be acted on in the office or the store. I commend this thought to those in this community, and to those in this congregation, if there are any, who are concerned, either as buyers or sellers, in Sunday trading. The answer has been made to me by certain tradesmen that they cannot afford to close on Sunday. The others would keep open, and these would lose their trade, and then "What shall we do for the hundred talents?" Things are said sometimes by Christian men, that would sound very queer, indeed, if said in this place.

In all such cases, when Christian principle is at variance with apparent self-interest, we might reply as the prophet did to Amaziah, "The Lord is able to give thee much more than this," and any man takes a business risk, as well as a moral risk, who disregards the laws of Him Whom he believes to be the providential Governor of the universe. And the reply would be appropriate. No man is the loser, in the long run, for obeying the commands of God as recognized by his own conscience. But while this is true, and is a safe and wise principle to act upon, we are not to infer, because God is able to make good a worldly loss that might ensue on obedience to Him, that therefore He will do it. His plans for us are further reaching than that. For conceive a state of things in which righteousness should be always profitable for this world. What room would there be for the exercise of faith? What temptation to the choice of evil? What virtue in the choice of good? What test of our willingness to obey? Religion would become a matter of calculation, and the most selfish of mankind would be, to all outward seeming, the most obedient to God.

Nay, rather let us be thankful that the moral Governor of the universe has ordained trials of principle; that He has lifted us out of the narrow circle of present interests by holding out to us, as motives, remote and not immediate results; that He develops our spiritual manliness by calling us to make sacrifices for principle; that He teaches us the supreme motive of *duty, pure and simple;* that in a thousand ways and instances the question comes up before us for decision, sharp and definite: A clear conscience? Or a hundred talents?

2. This same short-sighted worldly policy also it is which often leads men of whom we should expect something better to adopt false principles and methods in sustaining what appears to them the cause of truth and right, in

politics, sometimes in social reforms, and even in religion. In both these we find right-hearted men doing that, under a mistaken idea of its necessity, which they would not attempt to justify on any other ground. They appeal to the passions, the prejudices, the party-spirit of men; they employ the unholy weapons of misrepresentation, of invective, of corruption, thinking in their foolish worldly-wisdom, that they are doing God or their country service—doing acknowledged evil, indeed, but doing it "that good may come."

So thought those Roman Catholic priests in New York, a few years since, who promoted gambling at the Cathedral Fair as a means of raising funds for the service of the Church. And so thought Amaziah. In going against the Edomites he was fighting the Lord's battles, and it was very important that the Lord's battles should be fought. To be sure there were objections to the plan of hiring idolatrous mercenaries, but then it was extremely doubtful if the Lord's cause could be sustained without them, and of course it had to be sustained.

Now when people recognize the fact that a certain mode of attaining good ends is wrong or doubtful, and yet adopt it because it seems necessary, they need to be reminded of several considerations.

They need to be reminded *that God rules.* "God hath power to help and cast down." If

He hath not, then He is not God. "The lot is cast into the lap, but the whole disposing thereof is from the Lord." Instead, therefore, of undertaking to help Providence by doubtful means, their true course is to use all lawful and proper means, and then ask Providence to help them.

They need to be reminded, further, that in the progress of great movements, principles, and a consistent adherence to them, are of more consequence than methods. If our minds are possessed and elevated with the thought that the cause we desire to promote is a Divine cause, and this is the true view to take in every matter, in Church and State, in which we engage because we believe it to be right and true—we shall be less disposed to adopt unworthy means to promote it than if we limit our view to any of its details, the support of this man or that line of policy. But selfishness and narrowness intrude everywhere, and men become anxious for the success of a cause because they have adopted it and are identified with it. Their personal consequence, so to speak, is concerned in its success, and if matters do not go right just where they themselves are immediately interested, they find little comfort in their progress elsewhere. And so the means they take to promote them partake rather of the pettiness of the agent than of the dignity of the object, of the littleness of man rather than of the greatness of God. But faith in the truth, and faith in God, and a strict adherence to His will, are worth more to any good cause than a hundred talents.

The issue of Amaziah's experiment will show us, in regard to all schemes of worldly policy, that in the highest sense of prosperity they will not prosper. Even if they succeed in their main design, depend upon it there will be something wrong somewhere. They have left God out of view, and what can we do without Him in Whose favor is life? Amaziah listened to the admonition of the man of God and sent away the army of Israel. Here was a tardy triumph of principle. But he was not relieved from all the consequences of his original error. We read that "the army of Israel returned home in great anger," and "the soldiers of the army that Amaziah sent back, that they should not go with him to battle, fell upon the cities of Judah, from Samaria even unto Beth-horon, and took much spoil." From allies they had become enemies. An illustration, this, of the inevitable danger of tampering with what is wrong. Before an action we have its consequences in our power, but not after it. How does this consideration show the folly of short-sighted beings like ourselves deciding questions involving a principle on the ground of mere expediency! Is it expedient? How can we tell whether it is expedient until we know all its consequences? Ours is a simpler duty to ask whether it is right or not, and leave the results to God.

WORLDLY POLICY.

This last incident in the narrative suggests further a lesson for those—and who has not at times found himself in such a position?—for those who become conscious that they have taken a false step, and are hesitating whether to advance or to retreat from it. Under the circumstances what is best to be done? It is certainly bad to have gone so far, but it is possible to go further and fare worse—to become more deeply involved in the difficulties and embarrassments of wrong-doing. You can never recover yourself entirely; no sin, and, sad to say, no error, goes altogether unpunished; but you may in a measure retrieve the future. Amaziah paid dearly for having brought the army of Israel into his kingdom, but to have kept it there might have involved his utter ruin.

Worldly policy, then, is not even politic; and that only is truly *expedient* which is truly *right*.

The time will come in all our lives when the lessons of Amaziah's history are very practical lessons for us to ponder. To most of us it has come, and will come again—the time when duty and principle seem to be on one side in some marked emergency and self-interest and expediency on the other. It would be easy to be virtuous if virtue and immediate and apparent prosperity went always hand in hand. But times of adversity, and especially critical times, times when everything is trembling, and the future is uncertain, and results of present action difficult to be foreseen—these are times when men need to be anchored to the rock of principle. Business men have frequent occasion to know how unstable men are in emergencies. But it is a miserable mistake for a man to go about on the low ground of expediency. Let him get on the high ground of principle, and see where *the right* lies. What is the faith good for that cannot trust Providence farther than itself can see? How simple the lesson, and yet, apparently, how hard to learn, that the approbation of God is worth more to any man than a hundred talents; worth more to any cause than 100,000 men.

We can easily see that the whole difficulty with Amaziah was that he had not faith enough in God. "He sitteth upon the circle of the heavens, and all the inhabitants of the earth are as grasshoppers." Yet of this great Being the Eternal Word hath said that He numbers the very hairs of our head. In all emergencies let us have faith in God—the faith that goes hand in hand with obedience—and serve Him, not like Amaziah, hesitatingly, regretfully, unwillingly, but boldly, generously, uncompromisingly, because confidently, "with a perfect heart."

Contrast the Amaziah type of Christians with their opposites. As to the former, they are doubtful and uneasy, constantly looking into the future, and troubling themselves about the consequences of their actions, which, if they are satisfied that they are right, is no business of theirs. They have no strong and simple and child-like faith, and so they have but little comfort in religion.

How different the man who is actuated by a whole-hearted religious spirit! His aim is simple —he seeks to know the will of God in order that he may do it. How straightforward he is! How frank and fearless! How contented and comfortable he is, with the faith of a child in his Father. He meddles not in things too high for him, but is content to do his known duty, and leave God to take care of His own cause and of him.

PRAYER.

S. JOHN'S, STAMFORD, AUGUST 17, 1873.

PRAYER:

A LAW OF THE NATURAL AND OF THE SPIRITUAL WORLD.

"If ye then, being evil, know how to give good gifts unto your children, how much more shall your Father which is in heaven give good things to them that ask Him?"—ST. MATTHEW vii. 11.

"O Thou that hearest prayer, unto Thee shall all flesh come."—PSALM lxv. 2.

I. *Prayer is the instinctive appeal of weakness to power.** It is a spontaneous thing—a natural cry, like the cry of pain, forced out of us when we are off our guard, even if it be repressed at other times—when our "soul melteth away because of the trouble," then we "cry unto the Lord in our trouble, and He delivereth us out of our distress." We are born with the instinct of prayer—when the child wants anything, he asks for it; there is not one of us who has outgrown the idea of asking for what we want, and we never will. We may restrain ourselves, from pride, or for other reasons, but in so far as we do not ask for what we really and greatly desire, we are in an artificial state, and not a natural. And just so soon as a child grasps the idea of a

---
* Bishop of Peterborough, I think.

God, he grasps the simplest idea of prayer to God—transferring it from his parents to One Who has larger powers than they. The idea grows and develops with his advancing intelligence, for as he provides more things for himself, his wants are still enlarged beyond himself, and he has continually to appeal to others. If he believes in God, his natural impulse is to pray to God.

And, moreover, see how all our training in life under God's natural laws of providence tends to promote dependence and asking. From the very beginning of our lives we have known but two ways of getting what we desire. If what we wanted was within our own power, we helped ourselves to it. If it was not within our power, we asked for it. At home, in our childhood, we did not ask others for what we could get for ourselves; or, if we did, our parents, if they were wise, did not give it to us. But anything that was good for us, and that we could not get for ourselves, they got for us, when we asked them. They encouraged work, and they encouraged prayer. This is the Divine order for the training of childhood—it has developed our self-reliance, our energy, our industry, our perseverance, all the qualities which tend to make us strong and efficient—it has also developed a finer, tenderer set of qualities, affection, trust, unselfishness, humility.

When does this training stop? And where?

When have any of us ceased to want things that we could not get for ourselves? When has our weakness ceased its appeal to power? The providential training for prayer is going on still in all of you. When you want a physician to cure you, you ask him—you appeal to his superior power, superior, *i.e.,* relative to your power in that matter. Whenever you want any exertion of superior skill or power for your benefit, you ask it. If you cannot pay for it, no matter; you ask it still, if you very much need it, and have any reason to believe that asking will get it for you. In your relations to government, for instance, how you prize the right of petition—what an outrage the subject has always felt it when the right of petition has been denied! It is felt to be a natural and inalienable right; so much so that never, so far as I know of history, has it even been made a matter of special statutory provision.

And why should this instinct of prayer, this natural right of petition, be supposed to stop with our relations to man? Imagine some superior being, not Divine, and yet more than human, whose knowledge of, and therefore whose power over nature was far greater than yours, who could help you when you wanted help, and when you could not get it from man—what would be your attitude toward such a being? Would it not be the attitude of prayer? Would you not naturally ask him for what you need?

But why stop there? Why not rise still higher with your desires, and let your requests be made "known unto God"? There is nothing, surely, in Divinity, to arrest this natural course of prayer.

We see, therefore, that prayer is a natural instinct, developed and encouraged by all our providential training under the natural and social order which God has established. What can we infer from this but that prayer was intended? And *if prayer is intended, then we must believe that answers to prayer are intended also.* For, otherwise there would be a failure in the correspondences of things which we find nowhere else. Every faculty and tendency of our nature has its response and counterpart in things around us; as the eye is made for light and light provided for the eye, as the appetite implies food, so this irrepressible human cry of prayer finds the Ear to hear it, and the Heart to be touched by it, and the Will to be moved by it, and the Hand to be stretched out to answer it. *Prayer is a law of the natural and of the spiritual Kingdom of God.*

II. But it is sometimes felt that it is unreasonable to think that God should be influenced by our desires, because of the greatness of God and His concerns, and the littleness of man and his concerns.

1. To this we reply, that if *a large idea of the greatness of God makes prayer difficult, a larger will make it easy.* For in any just conception of

the greatness of God, He is too great to be influenced by relative magnitudes. Greater and less are words without meaning as applied to what He is and does. They are finite conceptions, and He is Infinite. "He sitteth upon the circle of the heavens, and all the inhabitants of the earth are as grasshoppers. The nations are as the small dust of the balance before Him; He taketh up the isles as a very little thing." So far as His relation to them is concerned, the things that seem great or small to you are all to Him, equally great or equally small. Their importance, to Him, is measured by their importance to you, and what is not too small to interest you, is not too small to interest Him.

2. Moreover, why are we to suppose ourselves too insignificant to influence God with our desires ? "Consider the lilies of the field." "Two sparrows are sold for a farthing, yet not one of them falls to the ground without Him." "Ye are of more value than many sparrows." What is the evident purpose of nature? What does the world stand for?—*our* world ? In what do all the operations of nature culminate—these operations which He orders and regulates with unceasing care—but in man ? Man is the apex and crown of all earthly things, and what concerns him is important—more important than anything else. And, moreover, what do we or can we ask God to do for us that is larger than what He actually does? "The life is more than meat."

He has given us life. Will He stop at the meat? "The body is more than raiment." He has made our bodies. Will He draw the line at raiment? The greater includes the less.

III. Up to this point we have considered the question of the reasonableness of prayer and the probability of answers to it, and have answered it out of the abundant teachings and analogies of nature. But we who are here accept the Bible as a revelation of God, and therefore I proceed to ask, whether there is anything in the representation God gives of Himself and His relation to us in the Bible, that may lead us to expect that He should be influenced by our requests.

1. Does it appear from revelation that we are insignificant?

Christ said some strong words on this point, to the effect that the whole world is valueless in comparison with a single human soul, and the whole world "includes the order of nature." And the Scripture teaches us why we are so valuable. We are made "in the image of God." We shall endure when the fixed heavens are rolled together as a scroll, and the firm earth is shrivelled and consumed. We can be companionable to Him. For our redemption He has given His Son, and "if God spared not His Son, but delivered Him up for us all, how shall He not with Him also freely give us all things?"

2. And again, what does God in Scripture teach us concerning His present relation to us?

Our Lord declares it incidentally to this very argument, "If ye then, being evil, know how to give good gifts unto your children, how much more shall *your Father which is in heaven* give good things to them that ask Him." We are not orphans in a relentless world. We have a Father and He rules it. "Like as a father pitieth his own children, even so the Lord pitieth them that fear Him." What does this relation imply? It implies care on His part. It implies prayer on ours. For what sort of a family would that be in which the children could not ask for what they want, and the father would never grant it?· And, on the other hand, what sort of a family would that be in which the children got everything they asked for? It is not that sort of family into which you and I have been born, and in which we are being reared and nurtured as "the sons and daughters of the Lord God Almighty."

3. Recognizing this relation, then, between God and ourselves, let us ask, What effect will prayer naturally have on this relation? Why should He so arrange things that His people should pray? What are the uses of prayer, as He would see them? And, by *prayer,* let us understand the real desires of His children, spoken or unspoken. For the lifting up of the heart to our Heavenly Father is *prayer.*

a. The first and most obvious use of prayer is, that it brings His children into His presence for direct intercourse with Him. If he had, as

He might have, established the order of events, so that everything which was best should happen in due course, we should never have occasion to approach Him personally.

We could not appeal to laws and forces, and hold affectionate and trustful communion with them; and if these, *as we understand them*, were the fixed, inflexible media of His action for us and on us, our minds would never look beyond them. And O how our best affections would pine and wither for want of an object to which our hearts could bring and offer them.

It would be like a family in which nurses and governesses did everything for the children, and the father and the mother were remote and cold—powers, indeed, back of everything, but in no immediate personal relation; nay, it would be worse, as if the feeding and clothing, and guiding and teaching, were done by some sort of machinery; and the child should stretch out its hand for a loving hand, and look for an eye, a loving eye, in vain, and pine for a breast on which to nestle. O, how orphaned you and I would feel, if we never could look up into our Father's face, and pray! For a certain conscious relation springs up between the suppliant and the Giver, which is a joy and comfort to both, producing love, producing trust, and holding a prophecy of the eternal happiness of eternal and unhindered companionship. Is this a desirable relation, worth establishing and confirming? You, who pray habitually, know that it is.

b. Another use of prayer is, that it teaches us our dependence. Suppose we never needed anything except what we could get for ourselves. Suppose that, instead of being born helpless infants, we came into the world full-grown, able to get what we want, to stand up for ourselves, and take care of Number One. What a selfish, ill-conditioned, angular, uncomfortable set of people we should be, every man looking on his own things, and not on the things of others. Human society would be intolerable. And we should stand up before God as we stand up before men, with no reverence, and no humility. And, in fact, men are lacking in reverence and humility just in proportion as they forget their dependence upon God. But when a man prays, it makes him feel his dependence, and if he is dependent, it is best that he should feel it. If he says, every morning, "Give us this day our daily bread," he is likely to remember, from time to time during the day, that while he is working, God is giving him life and strength to work, and he grows humble and thankful.

c. And still another use of prayer is, that it subdues our imperative desires into submission. When we come into the presence of God with our minds made up, and our desires eager that what we think best should come to pass, we are brought, in prayer, to feel that He rules, and ought to rule, and that we must make up our minds accordingly. Is not this a result of prayer? Let any one ask himself what has been his experience, when he has had some urgent desire upon his mind, and felt that it *must* be answered, or he could not endure. Something, perhaps, for himself, which he has set his heart upon having, or doing, or being, and which, if he cannot have, or do, or be, the sweetness of life is all taken out of it, and he feels as if he could never care for anything again. But while he kneels, beginning ever so importunately, there comes in upon him by slow and imperceptible degrees the conviction that God rules, that the matter is not in his own hand, and it is best it should not be; that He to Whom he calls for this is wise, and loving, not a God afar off, uninterested in the suppliant's concerns, but very near, and very sympathetic with what is true, and honorable, and real, in his desires; and, somehow, he rises from his knees with the feeling that if this thing should not be, after all, he could bear it, with God's help. Not all at once submission will come, but it will grow.

Or perhaps you pray for another—for the recovery of some one very dear to you from pain and sickness. You begin, anything but submissive, and when you try to contemplate the possibility of denial, and say, "Thy will be done," it seems as if you cannot get it out. But it must come out, you know that very well, and somehow or other, after you have been in that loving Presence a while, and the awful majesty of Infinite Power and Infinite Wisdom, made warm and tender by the consciousness of Infinite Love, settles down upon your spirit; you feel that you and yours are children—that He knows and cares—and you can leave it there. Submission grows as the demands upon it increase—"Though He slay, yet will I trust in Him."

Or it may be that your desire has had, so far as you could see, the honor of God, or the purity and progress of the Church, or some great question of right, mixed up with it, so that you invoked God almost peremptorily to make bare His arm, and interfere, and vindicate the cause that was no less His than yours, even as Elijah did against the idolatries of Israel. And while you have prayed, you have been led to feel how much of human passion and self-will has mingled with your seemingly unselfish prayers, and when you had looked in vain for Him in earthquake and fire, He has answered in the still, small voice, and bade you be still, and wait His time for interposition, for that He saw further than you, and would act in due time. Have you not thus learned submission often in the very act of prayer?

d. And another use of prayer is that it teaches obedience. Obedience, in the first place, to the natural law of work, for nobody ever yet truly prayed without doing what he could to bring about the fulfilment of his prayer. As the Bishop of Melbourne once said when setting forth a special prayer in time of drought, "Prayer will not answer as a substitute for irrigation." And, let me add, the prayer for the sick will not answer as a substitute for good sewerage; nor is it a substitute for the doctor, or for disregard of his directions. If anybody says that praying for what he wants tends to make a man neglect working for it, then those who pray habitually know that he speaks out of a theory, and not out of his experience. Prayer promotes obedience to all God's natural and moral and spiritual laws.

These are some of the reflex influences of prayer—the results to the character and spiritual habitudes of him who prays. Prayer, we see, is a means of bringing us into habitual intercourse with God, and making us dependent, humble, submissive, and obedient. Now if God is a Father, and we His children, do we not see reason in these uses of prayer, why He should ordain it, and make it a very necessity of our moral being? But observe, prayer has this reflex influence, *because it has direct efficacy.* If it be not a mode of influencing God, it is not even a mode of influencing ourselves. For if it is not directly efficacious—that is, if, when we pray, we do not expect to receive what we ask for, but only to make ourselves humble, reverent, submissive, then we shall, most assuredly, never pray at all. If we pray, it must be in the belief that, as we know how to give good gifts unto our children, so our Father which is in heaven *knows how to give good things to them that ask Him.*

5. There is one further point which I wish we might well consider before we close—*the moral impossibility of making any distinction in practice between prayer for physical and prayer for moral and spiritual results.* I suppose there are few among those who on scientific grounds deny the efficacy of prayer in what they call changing the order of natural events; and fewer still among those who simply doubt it, who would doubt or deny the influence of prayer on the spiritual life. But I venture to say that, however the two things may be separated in theory by those who do not pray, *in the practice of those who do pray it is impossible to draw the line.* The same prayer which contains the petition, "Forgive us our trespasses," contains also the petition for "daily bread." And when we pray to be delivered from evil, how can we help including the temporal with the spiritual possibilities of evil? And moreover we are so much and so inevitably influenced in moral and spiritual things by the state of our bodies, and by the circumstances which surround us, that the very prayer for spiritual things may as much involve physical changes as any prayer we can offer directly for

physical results. We pray "Lead us not into temptation," and the prayer is answered by bringing us into poverty or sickness, or by making it necessary for us to change our abode. Here, then, are a large number of persons, converted from the evil lives their natures tend to, living in the constant practice of prayer, and receiving, as they believe, and with reason, constant answers to prayer in the increase of their spiritual life. The better Christians, the more they pray. Is it not a moral impossibility that they should arrest their prayers at once the moment they touch the confines of "the order of nature," and refrain to ask for the less when they have received the greater? Is it not natural that they should ask, in some surprise, of those who would warn them off from this as a forbidden region of prayer, in words that were used of old, "Whether is easier to say, 'Thy sins be forgiven thee,' or to say, 'Arise, and walk'?"

Is the spectacle on which the mind's eye of the disbeliever and doubter rests with content, a conceivable one to the great body of mankind, the spectacle of a world handed over to a dreadful Fate (for such is the alternative to a prayer-hearing God) of myriads of anxious souls looking up into impenetrable skies, vainly assaulting heaven with prayers which only fall back again like stones to the feet of them that send them? You cannot arrest the ejaculations of a sorrowing, suffering, sinning race, bursting forth from hearts instinct with prayer, under sudden pressure of temptation, or danger, or pain, or springing ever upward spontaneously and habitually from spirits trained to pray. What a world this would be— it cannot be described—a prayerless world ! If it could be drawn, it would be a picture none of us would care to look upon. The difficulties, apparent on the surface, of believing the doctrine and the duty of prayer, are far less than the difficulties, increasing the more they are thought of in the way of denying it. It is the hopefullest voice of a sad humanity, having no hope in itself, and nothing to hope from things around it. "O Thou that hearest prayer, unto Thee shall all flesh come !"

THE PURGING OF THE FLOOR.

S. JOHN'S, STAMFORD, DECEMBER 7, 1890.

THE PURGING OF THE FLOOR.

"Whose fan is in His hand, and He will thoroughly purge His floor, and gather His wheat into the garner; but He will burn up the chaff with unquenchable fire."—ST. MATTHEW iii. 12.

"For judgment I am come into this world."—ST. JOHN ix. 39.

If you should go into the outskirts of a village in Palestine during the harvest season, you would notice a number of circular spaces of ground, from fifty to one hundred feet in diameter, very level and smooth, with a closely-cut sward, if any, upon which men, horses, and oxen are busily at work. These are the threshing-floors, and they are now much as they have been, in that land of unchanging habits, since the days when the sons of Jacob made grievous mourning for him at the threshing-floor of Abad, and the threshing-floor of Araunah, the Jebusite, was bought by King David at a price for the site of the Temple.

During the day the sheaves of wheat have been brought thither by the harvesters, and spread upon the level ground, and trodden out by the feet of unmuzzled oxen, or more effectually crushed by the passage over it, round and round, of a sort of flat sledge, on the under sur-

THE PURGING OF THE FLOOR.

face of which are ribs of iron, or small, rough stones, or spikes, inserted in rollers—the "new sharp threshing instrument having teeth," referred to in Isaiah (Chapter 41). When this has been sufficiently done, and the larger straw thrown out from the floor, the wheat and chaff remain—and now, towards the end of the day, when the evening breeze springs up, the workers take large wooden shovels, and with them toss up the mingled mass into the air in such wise that the wind carries the chaff away, and the heavier grain drops down to the floor again. Finally, after being gathered into a large heap in the centre of the floor, the wheat is taken to the garners, and the chaff is collected and burned.

This throwing up the chaff and grain for the wind to separate them is the primitive process of winnowing, and what is referred to in the text as the "fan" is simply the large wooden shovel with which they are thrown up against the wind. And this primitive process of winnowing it is that furnishes the illustration which John the Baptist uses to indicate the mission of the Christ in this world of mingled good and evil, "Whose fan is in His hand, and He will thoroughly purge His floor, and gather His wheat into the garner; but He will burn up the chaff with unquenchable fire"—unquenchable, because of the fierce flame with which the dry stuff burns until it is burnt out.

THE PURGING OF THE FLOOR.

What the Forerunner thus announced as the mission of the Christ, the Christ Himself declares to be His mission in the world in the second of the verses which I have read: "For judgment I am come into this world"—judgment, not merely in the sense of passing sentence—the word, rendered judgment, means discrimination, separating, making evident the distinctions between things. As in a chemical compound the introduction of a third element precipitates one of the others, and so separates them according to their essential qualities, so the Christ, His principles, His kingdom, come into human society, and forthwith men range themselves on one side or the other; they accept or reject Him, and then fall into their own place.

But before going any further, let me say that we shall greatly broaden and enrich our conceptions of the mission of the Christ to the world if we will but take in the thought that every good principle, and every beneficent and righteous movement that ever is, or ever was, or ever will be, is part of His kingdom, is His cause, is identified finally with Him and His redemptive work for the whole race of mankind. He is "the Saviour of all men, specially of them that believe"—the good in all men is their often unrecognized derivation from Him Who came to rescue all men and all things from the evil that else would dominate them. This is the religious view of things, and the worthy one, that *every* good and perfect gift is from above, that every good cause is the cause of Christ, and every righteous impulse in men springs eventually out of the new life that He has brought into humanity. You cannot really divide goodness into natural and supernatural—all goodness is Godness, and the difference between the religious man and others is that one recognizes where it comes from, and consciously puts himself into sympathy with it as from God, and of God, while the other, at best, thinks only of the thing itself, and its harmony with his own best thought and feeling.

Now here we are in a world like the threshing-floor, on which is a commingled mass of good and evil, of the valuable and the worthless, the wheat and the chaff of things. But the Kingdom of Christ is organized in the world to test and separate the good and the evil, to bring out the true characters of men and things. It is a disturbing force, it stirs things up, it enters like the third element into the chemical compound, and there is a clouding of the hitherto clear liquid, there is a ferment made, but after a while the combination is dissolved, one of the two originally inert elements is precipitated, and it is seen which is which.

Or, to recur to the main illustration, Christ in His kingdom takes the fan, and plunges it into the mingled mass of wheat and chaff which make up human affairs, and throws it up into the wind, and the chaff is blown away, and the heavier and worthier grain falls to the floor again —the good is separated from the evil. As I have often said here, the Kingdom of God is organized righteousness—organized, because effective work calls for organization of moral and spiritual forces to do it. The Church of Christ, which is here to carry on His work, is not like the stupid ox, treading aimlessly over wheat and chaff together, but like the intelligent man, whose definite purpose is to identify and divide them, throwing them up in cloudy confusion into the air, where the discriminating wind of God may catch them, and let the clear grain fall together.

And so the Church of Christ is to be the assertor and vindicator of all right principles, the strong supporter of all righteous movements in society—it is not to be stolidly indifferent to moral distinctions, nor to rest contented with the admixture of the evil and the good which it cannot wholly and immediately help. It is to be a disturber of the public peace, to be nobly discontented with things as they are, to try and get the evil out of them that is now in them. For Christ said, "I came not to send peace on earth, but a sword"—the sword now, the peace in the end—"first pure, then peaceable," is the Apostle's description of the Christian state.

Note the relation of John the Baptist's work to Christ's. He gathered the sheaves into the threshing-floor, the multitudes flocked to hear

THE PURGING OF THE FLOOR.

him, but there was as much chaff as wheat there, and he began the threshing process; he set their consciences to work, preaching the baptism of repentance, representing thus for all time the preliminary work of the Church in calling men to repentance, breaking the husk of habit. Meanwhile God's processes of providence and grace goes on. He deals with men by His *tribulum* or threshing instrument of tribulation. The word "tribulation" signifies just the pressing and grinding of hearts that are shut up to themselves and their own chosen belongings, as the rough-bottomed sledge is drawn round and round over the wheat in the husk. And then, when the husk is opened, and the time has come, He has His people tested. Emergencies arise for them. He takes them up and exposes them to His spiritual influences, which are as the wind that bloweth where it listeth, and their chaff is blown away, and the wheat in them remains on the threshing-floor and is carried at last into the garner. And the intelligent workman who is God's agent in this spiritual husbandry is the Christian Church, not *making* the difference between good and evil, but *bringing out* the difference, putting things in their true light, bringing men into contact with spiritual forces, applying means to effect God's moral and spiritual ends with men.

And now, leaving for a moment the illustration which has served a good purpose for us,

THE PURGING OF THE FLOOR.

but keeping in mind that the work of Christ and His Church is *the assertion and vindication of good and true principles*, that the Church and its principles *stand for all good*, and that they test and discriminate men, and things, and movements, let us see how the test is applied in the common and public concerns of men.

There are many points in the action of civil society at which the right and the wrong ought to be distinguished and dealt with as they deserve. The personal ministry of Christ on earth was passed amidst a condition of things which, if it had continued and developed, would have brought the world to moral and every other kind of ruin. But He put a set of principles into the world, and established an organization to maintain them in the world, which rescued it, and still are the basis of its moral life. *Christianity now is righteousness*—there is no getting behind that fact. It is the moral standard and test for men. Its principles are regulative. But not without opposition. A right principle, strongly and opportunely asserted, creates a ferment. But it precipitates the evil, brings it out so that it can be distinguished. And from time to time right principles are asserted, come to the front, raise a controversy and triumph, or are defeated, and try again. They test men, they test policies, they test public movements. This is a continuous process. It is God's working in the community —history shows that it is a beneficent and an effectual working. The world will never stagnate while there is a difference between right and wrong. The tossing of the ocean keeps it pure. Thank the Christ Whose fan is in His hand, when wrong comes to light.

The same is true in a thousand instances in the social life and habits of a community. There is a commingling of good and evil, quietly, unchallenged, until some test question arises, and then people *must* take sides. It makes confusions, heart-searchings, alienations, sometimes, but it cannot be avoided—the wheat and the chaff are thrown up together, and the wind of God separates them.

The test is applied often in the Christian community itself, within the very sphere of Church action. The Church is tempted to worldliness. Low principle, unworthy methods, selfish motives, are brought from time to time into strong contrast with essentially Christian principles. Nothing is ever undertaken by and for the Church but the world, the flesh, and the devil put in their oar to swerve it a little, and to wreck it if they can. How often, for example, has that essential law of Christ's Kingdom to be re-asserted in the face of selfishness, that the Church is missionary—that it stands, not for its own sake merely, but for the honor of God and the benefit of the world! How hard it is to keep Christian people up to that principle! How the dry husk of materialism, in a thousand instances, shuts

THE PURGING OF THE FLOOR.

in the living and expanding faith of Christians! How much "tribulation" we all have to go through in order to enter fully and heartily into the true spirit of the kingdom of God!

And this leads to an obvious application of the thought of the text to the individual character. The fact is, that we all have wheat and chaff mingled in us, and they are not completely separated in us to the end of our days. We are not yet ready for the garner. The winnowing process is going on. Test questions come up from time to time, which make us sad with self-knowledges. In the details of each personal life Christ is continually judging us, by His Spirit and His Church pressing us to practical decisions in conduct and so in character. Questions, as we say, "come up." You are lying quiet, accepting, it may be, conventional standards of Christian duty; but something or somebody brings the question up, and you cannot escape it. How will you decide it? There is a state of suspense; pros and cons urge themselves; conscience and inclination are in controversy, and your decision cannot but show where you belong. God send you the gracious breath of His Spirit to blow the chaff away!

It is a comfort to know that He, not we, will gather the wheat into the garner. We might mistake. We often do misjudge. We apply arbitrary tests; He applies real ones. There is more true faith in many men than we imagine;

more faith in men who are not members of the Church, often, than they themselves imagine, for they and we are apt to apply conventional tests—to think that certain approved forms of experience, certain modes of expressing faith, are alone conclusive. I am persuaded that there are many men who do not believe in their own faith, who do yet believe in God. "He who, when goodness is impressively put before him, exhibits an instinctive loyalty to it, starts forward to take its side, trusts himself to it; such a man has faith, and the root of the matter is in such a man." (*Ecce Homo.*) The husk that shuts in that man's faith, and kindles its expansion and development into the full Christian life may be conventional irreligion, or the mere habit of being outside. Just as, sad to say, the husk that smothers another man's true spiritual life may be conventional religion, or the mere habit of being *inside.* Tribulation may be the necessary process for both. But *all* the wheat will get into the garner, and all the chaff will be consumed, thank God! And the final judgment by Him Who will come again in the might of His wisdom and love and righteousness and truth to judge the world, will be to separate the chaff from the the wheat, and put each where each belongs.

INSPIRATION AND ITS LIMITATIONS.

WHIT-SUNDAY, S. JOHN'S, STAMFORD, MAY 13, 1894.

INSPIRATION AND ITS LIMITATIONS.

"When He, the Spirit of truth, is come, He will guide you into all truth."—ST. JOHN xvi. 13.

Though its Founder has passed away from earth, yet Christianity is a present fact and power. And that not by the mere momentum of an impulse given eighteen centuries ago, but in virtue of a living Spirit working through all its agencies to-day. To guide men into truth, to strengthen men for duty—this is the office of the Holy Spirit, just so long as human judgment is fallible and erring, and human purpose weak and frail.

And so it is fitting that we keep festival in His honor, "by Whose holy inspiration we think those things that are good, and by Whose merciful guiding we perform the same"; Who puts in operation all those spiritual forces which are intended to be the supreme power in us; Who is with us in every inner conflict between good and evil, the Helper of our infirmities, "the Lord, and Giver of Life."

The work of the Holy Ghost is summed up in one word, *Inspiration*. What is inspiration?

It is not something confined to the Holy Scriptures, and in virtue of which they become the word of God. It is not merely a past, but a present fact as well. For inspiration is *the inbreathing by the Spirit of God of life and power into the spirit of man.* The living, working force for good in the world is the Holy Ghost "Who proceedeth from the Father and the Son." The Inspirer—Inbreather of moral and spiritual vitality.

It is characteristic of all life that it tends to perfect forms, but circumstances modify its development. The tendency of a tree is towards shapeliness and fruitfulness, but its symmetry is impaired and its productive power diminished by unfavorable conditions of soil and climate and culture. And so of the physical life of man, there is some account to be given, in the conditions under which it has grown up, of every imperfect and abnormal human frame.

The life-giving operations of the Holy Ghost likewise follow this law, and here we find the reason for whatever of imperfectness appears in the communication of God to us, whether by His word, His Church, or by His influence on individual men. Inspiration is in itself sufficient for its purpose, but it is *influence*, and not *control*. In its practical working it meets with limitations which are human and earthly. Yet it accomplishes, substantially, what it sets out to do. The work of the Holy Ghost is not a failure. He has inspired the Bible. He still inspires the Church. He inspires also the individual Christian man.

INSPIRATION AND ITS LIMITATIONS.

These three modes of inspiration must be remembered when we speak of either of them, or else we get hold only of half-truths. The ultra-Protestant dwells only on the past inspiration of a Book, and so has hold of a half truth. The Romanist insists mainly on the present inspiration of the Church, and so *he* gets hold of a half truth. The Quaker, and the humanitarian also, hold that every individual man is directly inspired by the Divinity that fills the universe, and so he ignores Bible and Church, holding on to his half truth in turn. Put these half truths together, and you get the whole truth about the Holy Spirit's work in the world.

1. *Consider, first, His inspiration of the Bible.* I have used the common expression, but I cannot too strongly urge upon your remembrance what would correct much misunderstanding if it were remembered, that the inspiration is not in the books, *but in the men who write them.* The doctrine of the inspiration of the Book, and of every word and letter therein, came in with the Westminster Confession, was unknown to the early Church, and is not the doctrine of our own. That is expressed in the article, "Holy Scripture containeth all things necessary to our salvation," and is well put in the Collect, "Blessed Lord, Who hast caused all holy Scriptures to be written for our learning." If other Protestants had been contented with such intelligible and reasonable statements, the world would have been spared

INSPIRATION AND ITS LIMITATIONS.

much controversy, and much criticism, higher and lower. Revelation does not imply verbal inspiration.

But a sufficient revelation God has most assuredly given us, by the inspiration of the Holy Ghost upon the writers of Scripture. It was needful that He should make Himself known to men. We could not be left in ignorance of our own Father, for He claims our love and duty. We must know Him as a Person and His attitude and relation to us—that which of all things it most concerns us to know, and the knowledge of which our hungering hearts could never otherwise attain.

And yet, our knowledge of Him is not complete. How many perplexities and doubts we have! How many inexplicable things we find in Scripture—not enough to destroy our confidence and shake our trust in God, yet enough to trouble us. So many things "hard to be understood," that though through all the mists of uncertainty we can most of us behold His face in righteousness, yet we do wonder why it is not clearer.

The clouds that obscure the sun are earth born. Consider the conditions under which the revelation is given and received.

The instrument through which it is made to us is human speech. It is an inadequate instrument, but the only available one. We have framed language with reference mainly to the uses of our ordinary life; it is the medium of exchange for every-day thoughts and feelings. With all its stretching it cannot be made to fully embrace those higher and infinite ideas which a communication with Divine things must necessarily suggest.

And then, again, this revelation is not written on the heavens by the finger of God. It comes through men as His agents—inspired men, but with all their own individuality. The personality of Paul, and Peter, and John, of David, and Solomon, and Isaiah, is on all that they have written. Doubtless it is better so. The best telescope is said to be that in which the light from the heavenly body comes not directly to the eye of the observer, but is reflected to it from the surface of a mirror. It may be that we see and know God better, *for our purpose*, as the knowledge of Him comes to us reflected from other human hearts and minds, which have been specially prepared for its reception and transmission. "We see through a glass, darkly," says St. Paul. The reflector is not perfect, but it is sufficient. We shall see "face to face" by and by, when all these limitations are removed. Whatever the reason, this is the fact, in the Divine order.

And perhaps the reason is not far to find. Our capacity is limited. Communications made to us must have some relation with the power we have to appropriate knowledge and make it practical—light may dazzle rather than illuminate. Knowledge now is for the sake of love and duty; in another world it grows from more to more, and we shall know as we are known. Knowledge for its own sake may have a meaning there.

These, then, are limitations of the Scripture revelation of God—the inadequacy of human speech, the personality of human agents, and our own limited capacity for Divine communications.

Yet, notwithstanding all, Scripture answers its purpose. To the mind that is humble and teachable, God reveals Himself, into the heart that is open, He pours the moving conviction of His love. "With this man will I dwell," saith God, "even with him that is of a contrite and humble spirit, and that trembleth at My word." The first qualification for knowing God is to have the honest purpose of love and duty. "If a man love Me, he will keep My words, and My Father will love him, and We will come unto him, and make Our abode with him." The Scriptures are a sufficient rule of faith and practice, and adequacy to the purpose is all we can look for here.

2. In the second place, What is meant by the inspiration of the Church?

It began on the Day of Pentecost, and we know from the record what it meant then. It was, in substance, a gift of power to do the ordained work of the Church in bringing men to the knowledge of God in Christ, in teaching them truth, and helping them to duty. The life and power of the Christian Church in all the ages stand in its continued inspiration by the Holy Ghost.

The inspiration of the Church! When we reflect, this is seen to be a very necessary and true belief. In the Creed, after we have said, "I believe in the Holy Ghost," we go on to say, "I believe in the Holy Catholic Church, the Communion of Saints, the Forgiveness of Sins," and the rest. They stand together. For, shall we say that the Church is not inspired? That she is a living Church, yet with no in-breathing of the life of God; that she lives by her own inherent vitality, or in virtue of power derived from some other and inferior source? She has the promise that she shall never fail, her purpose never be defeated. "Lo, I am with you alway, even to the end of the world." This is the manner of the Saviour's presence—by the continual gift of the Spirit. "I will not leave you comfortless, I will come to you. I will send you another Comforter, even the Spirit of truth, that He may abide with you forever." "When He is come, He will guide you into all truth."

Has this promise been fulfilled? Not, perhaps, according to our natural expectations. We would have had a society whose claim none could dispute; which should have fallen into no

INSPIRATION AND ITS LIMITATIONS.

error on any point; whose teachers should always have taught the perfect truth of God, which truth should always be perfectly exemplified in the lives of its members. It should have been true and equal to its mission as the one Catholic Church; its doors should have been by this time opened to all, and all should have entered into it and been saved.

If such is our ideal—and it may well be—then we are very sure that it has not been realized. The Church of Christ has been divided and broken. Its teachers have often erred and gone astray. Its members, sanctified and sealed with the seal of God, have often and much discredited their profession.

And all this no recent or exceptional thing. It has been so from the beginning. It was the case, we find, in the days of the Apostles, while yet they, and many others with them, were, as is plainly declared in Scripture, inspired. Envy and strife, divisions, partisanship, worldliness, coldness, formalism, indifference to the deeper realities of religion, error in doctrine, and viciousness of life—these things have been from the beginning, and we look in vain through history for the Church as it ought to be.

But all this, again, is the imperfectness of human instrumentality, impairing the efficiency of the Divine institution, and impeding the fulfilment of its beneficent design. The treasure was in earthen vessels. The councils of the Church have been fallible, and have often erred. Her ministers have been human, and therefore weak, unwise, and sinful. Her members—all we can say of them is that they have never been equal to their position. When we see how much the Church has not done, we are ready to pronounce it a failure.

But we look again, and see what it has done. That it has preserved among men the knowledge of the Triune God. That it has kept the original Scriptures, and the ancient creeds, and the Apostolic ministry. That in all these 1800 years men have been baptized into Christ; have been taught the elementary truths of God as Father, of sin, redemption, judgment; have been made to recognize the fundamental principles of morality invested with the sanctions of Divine law; have been taught a charity wonderful and strange to the natural man; have lived lives of holiness, and died in the confidence and comfort of a holy hope—all this shows the Christian society founded on the Day of Pentecost to have been no failure in its main design as towards men.

Nor yet as towards God. The Church has been, and still is, the one organization existing on the earth for the common worship of God, and her temples have been open, her festivals observed, the acceptable incense of worship has ascended from her altars. The glorious company of the Apostles, the goodly fellowship of the prophets, the noble army of martyrs, have praised Him. The holy Church throughout all the world has acknowledged Him. She has conveyed the gifts of God to men, she has presented the offerings of men to God. She has succeeded in promoting the glory of God, and in applying His truths to the hearts and lives of men—she has succeeded, even though with an imperfect success. The imperfectness is human, the success is Divine. It comes of the present and continued operation of the Spirit of God. I know no other way of accounting for the preservation of the Christian religion in the world, and the blessings which have followed it. The history of Christianity has always presented the aspect of a Divine power and life tending to express itself in a perfect Christian society, but restrained by the imperfections and limitations of the material out of which this society had to be formed.

3. There was then the original inspiration of the writers of Scripture. There is the continual inspiration of the Church as the witness and keeper of the Faith, and the channel of Divine grace to man. And lastly there is the inspiration of the individual Christian—the imparting by the Holy Ghost to every human soul of life and power to appropriate to itself the truth and grace of God.

Does this again seem a novel and startling statement, that there is an inspiration of the Holy Ghost vouchsafed to every man? It is

INSPIRATION AND ITS LIMITATIONS.

most true and evangelical. For as the writers of Scripture were inspired to write it, so are we inspired to read it and to live it. There is an answering operation within us to correspond with what has been done for us. Are we not conscious that the Bible comes to us as no other book ever comes, that it fits our spirits, so to speak, that as by one and the same hand the key is fitted to the lock and the lock prepared for the key, so is the truth to be apprehended and the capacity to apprehend imparted by the same Almighty power.

This is very far from that vain conceit that the inspiration of the individual is the supreme law to himself, that it overrides all external revelations, that the authority of the Church is nothing, and the authority of the Bible is nothing, when they seem to conflict with what he deems the higher law of his own convictions. But the basis of all true religion is a revelation. It comes to us from without. We are not called upon to originate a faith, but to receive, examine, inspect and obey authentic revelation; and for this we are qualified by the continual help of the Holy Ghost.

For, not only mental but moral qualifications are necessary in dealing with communications from God. Integrity of purpose, love of truth, and willingness to follow where it may lead, these are of more value than acuteness of intellect and soundness of judgment; these are the

INSPIRATION AND ITS LIMITATIONS.

single eye which if we have, our whole body shall be full of light. Humility brings us nearer to God than ability. Hidden often from the wise and prudent, Divine things are revealed unto babes. The Spirit teacheth us the deep things of God, so far as we are willing and competent to receive them.

We are greatly guarded from mistakes on the subject of inspiration when we remember two things: first, that the presence and work of the Holy Spirit is continuous, and second, that it is in such manner and measure as is proper and adequate for the purpose intended.

His presence is continuous. He did not inspire a book and then retire from the world. This period in which we live is the dispensation of the Spirit. He is to abide with us forever. He is the Source of our spiritual life. He beareth witness with our spirits. He "sanctifieth the people of God." He teaches us to pray, "the Spirit of grace and of supplication." "He maketh intercession for us." He helps us in our conflicts with evil. We are "strengthened with might by His Spirit in the inner man." He guides us into all the deepest truth we know.

And yet His influence is not an absolute control, but sufficient for its purpose, which is to impart to willing souls such certitude of truth as may guide them, and such grace as may strengthen them to do their duty. He is pouring light in upon us from every side when our eyes are open. We are not to be timorous and suspicious of any means of real knowledge as if it were unsanctified; we cannot slight it as unimportant.

Criticism, if it be reverent, may bring us helps from philology and history and science. Authority, if it be legitimate, may settle some doubtful questions by the voice of Christendom. Individual interpretation, if it be honest and devout, is entitled to respect and consideration.

For the original revelation was adequate to its main purpose, as inspired by the Holy Ghost. And by the operation of the same Spirit the Church has been, notwithstanding all its errors and imperfections, a living Church preserving the truth, and conveying to individual souls the strengthening grace of God. And we are made, by the same Spirit, competent to understand the Scriptures for all practical purposes. No honest seeker has failed to learn his duty there, and sufficient motive to obedience and love. We are not perfect Christians, but the Holy Ghost is working in us towards making of us the best that we can here become.

And this is all we should expect in a probationary condition. The question here is whether we have the germ and principle—the complete ideal is to be realized in the future. He is the Quickener of the germ of spiritual vitality.

"More life, and fuller, *that* we want,"
so that the service of God, worship, work, giving—all Christian sentiment and duty—shall be, not a drudgery, but a joy of living, and the earnest of a worthy immortality, an everlasting life worth living.

CHRISTIAN TRAINING.

THIRD SUNDAY IN ADVENT, ST. JOHN'S, STAMFORD, 1894.

CHRISTIAN TRAINING.

" What manner of child shall this be?"—ST. LUKE i. 66.

Such was the exclamation of the wondering "neighbors and cousins" assembled when John Baptist was admitted, by the rite of circumcision, to membership in the Jewish Church. Their enquiry was answered in the song of Zacharias, who with prophetic vision looked forward to the advent of yet Another, Whose forerunner his infant son should be: "And thou, child, shall be called the prophet of the Highest, for thou shalt go before the face of the Lord, to prepare His ways."

But the enquiry thus made is applicable to every child born into the world: "What manner of child shall this be?" For though there may be nothing specially noticeable about the infancy of children, we know there is an individuality which belongs to each, a germ which will develop into something that has no exact parallel anywhere. In some respects every child is unlike every other that ever has been born, or ever will be. Unlike in form and feature, unlike in temper and disposition, unlike in natural capacity and acquired ability, unlike in outward circumstance and in inward character. The same elements are there, but susceptible of infinite diversity in their combinations. We may say, if we choose, that this child will be like other children, and to a certain extent so he will—with like passions and propensities, like experiences, like influences, this child shall be in general like *all* children, but in particular like none.

There is room, therefore, for this enquiry; there is an uncertainty about the future of children. The prophetic eye might look over the children who sit here side by side, looking over the same Prayer Books, saying the same words of prayer, and trace their future course in lines of wide divergence. Of one he might predict, as of John Baptist, "Thou shalt go before the face of the Lord to prepare His ways, to give knowledge of salvation unto His people." On another he might look, and track him in an evil and unhappy course, and drop the veil before he looked too far. While before another he might see stretching out the dead level of an aimless and useless life, and then a departure hence, unnoticed and unregretted. It has been said: "We look upon an unconscious infant, and it is as it were a drop of water on the summit of the Andes. A pebble, the finger of a child, may turn it; but that moment decides whether it shall meet and mingle with the stormy Atlantic, or rest and glitter on the bosom of the broad Pacific." The illustration may serve to give us a conception of the uncertainty that hangs over the future of an infant's life, and the seemingly trivial causes which influence—though they never can decide, for nothing external can ever decide—its destiny. The starting of a life is of inexpressible importance, for who of us will venture to say when moral and spiritual influences commence to act, and when the shaping of the life begins? Much depends on that, but, thank God! not everything. Influences from above may fall—light and heat from the heavens —the light of God's converting truth, the warmth of God's converting love, and release any single drop in the stream of human life from the attraction of earthly influences, and lift it, and carry it over to the other side.

But no earthly analogy may express the unfathomable mystery of the human will. Here lies the main element of uncertainty in the child's future. *It is uncertain because he is free.* There is no such uncertainty in the lower forms of life. If the seed lives and develops at all, we know in substance what its development will be. We know what manner of tree it shall be, and that whatever modifies its size, or shape, or quality, is due to its environment of soil and climate and moisture, and not to any choice which itself has made.

But the child will be free to shape his course, to adopt or reject principles of faith and duty which will determine the character of his life.

This idea of human freedom lies at the basis of Christian training. There is no unseen and incalculable power overmastering human wills. There is no necessity upon any man which prevents his living the Christian life, so far as his knowledge extends. We can work hopefully in Christian training, bringing all healthful influences to bear. These cannot *secure,* but they can *promote* a right decision in the crises of life. The future of children can be so influenced by influencing the present, that *the Christian life will be the reasonable probability.*

This is a practical point, *the general efficiency of religious training.* In such training there are three principal elements.

1. At the basis of it all lies Baptism, the bringing the child into covenant with God. He is to be trained, not in order that he may *become* a Christian, but because he *is* one, and ought to continue such, "that this child may lead the rest of his life according to this beginning."

Consider the two-fold effect of Baptism. In the first place it has a moral effect—it brings the child within the environment of Christian influences. It brings him into his heavenly Father's earthly house and family. The Church is the kingdom of heaven upon earth, the household of God, and one purpose of the household is the training of the young. Those he finds around him are the members of Christ, in sympathy with his religious thought and life. He is in a spiritual atmosphere, subject to spiritual influences. He is taught that he has a place in God's kingdom, *that faith and duty are for him not simply at some future time, but now,* and progressively as he grows more and more capable for them. And this fact tends to make him receive readily, and as it were insensibly, Christian teachings and impressions. They come in upon him in a natural order, and in his impressible time, when everything he sees is right to him, and all he hears is truth, and anything other than the love and fear of God is an unthought-of thing. This is as it should be, and is a proper result of Baptism, and of the position into which Baptism brings the Christian child. I must use again the expression I have often used here: *The Christian position is the appointed means for bringing about the Christian disposition.* What a difference it makes that I can say to the children in our Sunday-school, children, you are here in your Father's family, you are God's children, signed and sealed as His, the mark of the cross is on your brow—now therefore try, with His help, which will most surely be given you, to live as you know His children ought to live. You are not outside, but inside the Christian Church.

And, being inside, under a promise of grace, they receive grace. Not irresistible grace, but grace to balance weakness with strength, and innate evil with infused good. They are at once in two worlds. The helpful influences of the spiritual world are set over against the hindering influences of the natural world, and they are free to choose between them. For this is the inward part or thing signified in Baptism, the touch of the Spirit of God upon the spirit of the child which makes it not an outward rite merely, but what our Saviour described it to Nicodemus, a baptism of water and the Holy Ghost, not separately, but together.

2. And so the second element in a true religious training is *the development of the sense of a responsibility already existing.*

The baptized child is not to wait until he is old enough to choose, before he enters on the Christian life. He is in it from the first. There is no time when he can say, I have made no profession of religion, therefore religious faith and duty is for me an open question. I am free. I mean to be a Christian some day, but for the present I will enjoy my freedom from obligation.

But such is not God's plan. Children are to grow up in the Church just as they grow up in the State, citizens from the first, with responsibilities proportioned to their capacities for fulfilling them. What should we think of the theory that a man is under no obligations as an American citizen because he was born into them and had not of himself assumed them? Such a principle would disorganize the State. So would it disorganize the Church.

All analogy teaches us that the order is, first duty, then doctrine ; first, submission to law, and then study and acceptance of the law. Ask a child whether he ought to obey his parents, and he will answer : Of course I ought. Ask him why, and he has never yet thought of the reason. This, in the family, in the State, and in the Church, is God's providential order.

3. A third element in Christian training is, *home teaching and example.*

This is one of those things the importance of which every one acknowledges, and almost every one forgets or undervalues. *Home teaching and example!* What strange ponderings must come often into children's minds when they take in the fact that their parents, or either of them, are unbaptized, or practically unreligious ! How there begins then that balancing of affections, and trusts, and convictions which weakens the faith and conscience of the young, and is so effective an ally to the world, the flesh, and the devil. Few men would be satisfied that their children should not be trained in the principles of the Christian religion, and, starting from Baptism, "lead the rest of their lives according to this beginning." Happy inconsistency, often, but always perilous !

By such a training, then, founded on the fact of Baptism, bringing out the sense of a present and not merely a future responsibility, and strengthened by the pervading influence of example, the uncertainty of the child's future may be lessened. It cannot be altogether removed. No amount of training can determine, it can only *influence* the future. For every one, at his years of discretion, must choose whether he will continue in the course he has begun, and abide in his Father's house wherein he was born again. God applies no constraining force to keep him there, and what grace cannot effect cannot be effected by education. But in general, we need not fear that Christian training will be labor lost. A large experience in the families of the Church shows that it is not.

And if this experience finds many exceptions, and young people do often get away from truth and right, still this early training is a strong influence to draw them back, and a help and guide to repentance and amendment of life. The standard of a true life can never be utterly lost from the consciousness of one who has been once taught it. It is not in vain that people have a clear idea of the Christian religion, and of their true relation to God and their neighbor, deep down at the bottom of their minds and memories, even while it fails to control their active life. Appeals to conscience have something to go upon. It is something, in the latter days of life, to know what repentance is and implies. Says the Baroness Bunsen, speaking of a lady of rank who had lived a bad life (Vol. i., p. *233*): "I am thankful to know that she expired in faith and peace. She had offended greatly, but she had repented, and it had been her habit of mind for years to seek pardon through Christ. She has had cause to bless the memory of her mother; had not notions of religion been instilled in childhood, after the life she has led she would hardly have been able to imbibe them."

A man of over four-score, in conversation with me in a neighboring parish a few weeks since, bore this strong and touching testimony: "I have heard in my life-time more than six thousand sermons, for I have always gone regularly to church; but, all together, they have not influenced me so much as the teachings I had on Sunday afternoons from the lips of my mother." He might have added, that the teachings were the key to the sermons.

I have said these things to-day because I am greatly exercised to find how largely the good old fashion of home-teaching of children has fallen into disuse, while the Sunday-school does so little to make good the deficiency. And that not because the idea of the Sunday-school is not a good one, but because it is charged with a duty to which, in the nature of the case, it is not equal, and because it is used as a substitute for home-teaching, rather than as a supplement to it. Few children now can find their way through the Bible as many of us were taught to find it; few can intelligently use their Prayer

CHRISTIAN TRAINING.

Books. What can we expect, when an hour a week, amid distractions, under the guidance often of immature teachers, with parents indifferent to their children's regularity, punctuality, and that home-study of their lessons which is the parents' opportunity, is all that the family will allow the Church to give to their instruction? And what can be more unsuitable than the spectacle, which is witnessed every Sunday by the congregation coming to church for the afternoon service, of three-fourths of the children of the Sunday-school going away from it?

It is an annual distress and discouragement to me, when I begin to prepare young candidates for Confirmation, to find how slight a basis of Christian training I have to go upon. I have seriously pondered as to how I might get the adolescent boys and girls into a week-day class for my personal instruction during the larger part of the year, in the principles and duties of the Christian religion. But even in the limited period of preparation for Confirmation, I find that parents are willing to let other things, social engagements, symphony concerts, and all sorts of things, hinder and distract the candidates; and I have but little hope that it would be possible for me to secure their attendance for the two or three years before and after Confirmation for the general training which at their age they ought to have. And the outcome is unintelligent Christians, untrained Churchmen and women, superficial thinking and feeling on the greatest of all subjects, and therefore a ready surrender of Christian faith and duty to the naturally welcome suggestions of unbelief in their young manhood or womanhood, when, as the phrase goes, "they begin to think for themselves," but in reality do not think, or have no guidance in their thinking. And then, later on, when nothingarianism is found to be so conspicuously empty of spiritual satisfaction, comes the temptation to fancy that in the surrender of thought and conscience to the guidance of Romanism they may find an easier and surer way of satisfying their spiritual appetencies. For people do not ordinarily go to Rome as the result of intellectual processes, nor are they often unbelievers from anything that can really be called intellectual compulsion. Intellectual honesty and moral earnestness, *on a basis of sound Bible and Church training*, will keep most people from both these harbors of indolence.

I utter this note of warning to members of the Church, that their children are not going to be as well-informed Christians and Churchmen as they are themselves, unless they take more pains about it, unless they second the efforts of the Church and the ministry to teach them, and unless they exhibit in their own lives, and in their domestic arrangements, the example of caring for these things supremely. Let some other things drop out from your busy and overdriven lives rather than this. "What manner of child shall your child be?" Is there any more concerning question for a Christian parent than this?

The seriousness of this enquiry which I press upon you to-day, words cannot fully express. It is not, What shall he *have?* but, What shall he *be?* The former is the point which the world makes. In its estimation he *is* according to what he *has*. This is a small estimate of humanity. Says Jeremy Taylor, "How much, then, is a man inferior to a gold mine!" It is not the estimate of the Scriptures: "A man's life consisteth not in the abundance of the things which he possesseth." What he *has* is matter of temporary concernment, "he shall carry nothing away with him when he dieth"; but what he *is*, is matter of eternal interest.

"What manner of child shall this be?" What—in relation to this world? What—in relation to the world to come? What shall he *be?* not, What shall he *seem?* What—in presence of his own conscience? What—in the sight of God, "Who searcheth the hearts and trieth the reins of the children of men"? What shall he be when temptation tries him, when sure-coming trouble is heavy upon him, when prosperity wears its seductive smile? What shall he be when he is himself his only company on the bed of sickness, with nothing to hide him from himself, and when no unreality can stand before his searching self-consciousness? What—in the hour of death? What—in the day of judgment?

The capacities of his being can no more be measured than can the eternity that is before him. We can conceive of no limit to the evolution of a human life and character; this present time is but the starting-point. I suppose there is a point where the Mississippi River can be spanned by the hand of a man. Yet this infant rivulet, bubbling there and tossing in the lap of its mother, is the Father of Waters. Greater still is the disproportion between the present and the future of this infant of whom we ask: "What manner of child shall this be?" For the great solemnity of human life is this: That the being who comes into existence at the birth of a child *never goes out of it.*

THE BURIAL SERVICE.

FIRST SUNDAY AFTER EASTER, S. JOHN'S, STAMFORD, APRIL 13, 1890.

THE BURIAL SERVICE.

"Earth to earth, ashes to ashes, dust to dust; looking for the general Resurrection in the last day, and the life of the world to come."—(THE ORDER FOR THE BURIAL OF THE DEAD).

There are two ways of regarding death, the way of sentiment and the way of religion. That is, we may look at the subject through the medium of feeling, or through the medium of faith.

Both these modes of regarding it are legitimate, and are not inconsistent with one another. Indeed, we cannot enter into the comfort of the Christian view of death, except we first pass through the way of natural human feeling. We are men before we are Christians. "Howbeit," says the Apostle—and it is a principle of wide application—"that was not first which is spiritual, but that which is natural, and afterward that which is spiritual."

Both natural sentiment and Christian faith find their expression in the Burial Service of the Church; and I believe it is in part owing to this combination in "The Order for the Burial of the Dead" that it is, what it is so often felt to be, the most comforting service of the kind that we ever hear. Inconsolable and unreasoning, indeed, must be the grief that refuses to listen to such words as these. And though, in the shock and stun of the first days of bereavement, no words can satisfy short of such words of power as were uttered of old, "Young man, I say unto thee, Arise!" yet even then this service falls soothingly, and holds a germ of consolation which we know will ripen by and by.

It will be in harmony with the thought of the season, and with the services of the day, if we shall trace this morning the principle on which the Burial Office is constructed.

Let us observe, before considering the Office itself, how its use is regulated by the rubric, and who they are for whom it is appointed to be said. The rubrical direction is as follows: "Here it is to be noted that the Office ensuing is not to be used for any unbaptized adults, any who die excommunicate, or who have laid violent hands upon themselves."

From this it appears that this particular Office is designed for all those who, by their own act, or by the care of parents and sponsors, have been made by Baptism members of the visible Christian Church, and for no others. It is not hence to be inferred that no religious service is to be used at the burial of persons not baptized, but only that the manner of such service is left to the discretion of the minister, and that he is not bound, unless he sees fit, to officiate at all.

THE BURIAL SERVICE.

But no inference is to be drawn, from the use of this service, in favor of the moral and religious character of those who are baptized, nor adverse to the character of those who are not. Its use is not a question of character at all, it is simply a question of position. As to character, no man can venture infallibly to judge, and at such a time no man would willingly undertake to do so; but the fact of membership in the visible Church is one that can be definitely ascertained. In a Christian community, at any rate in our own congregations, it may usually be taken for granted that persons are baptized; and if they are not, it may then be taken for granted that those who have deliberately declined the responsibilities of Church membership would make no claim to its privileges. There are funeral rites appropriated to members of the Masonic Order, which are not used for others. Soldiers alone are buried with the honors of a military funeral —a civilian, however brave and loyal, may not claim them. In like manner the Church has provided an order for the burial of her own dead.

All who have given in their definite and formal adhesion to Christ, who have been sealed with the seal of discipleship, and thus admitted as citizens in the visible Kingdom of God in the world—for them the Church provides that unless they leave the Church by excommunication, or the world and the Church together by deliberate suicide, thus dying in the act of wilful sin, these words of faith, and hope, and comfort, shall be said over their graves.

And she provides no other. She knows no distinctions among her children, of high and low, of rich and poor. She

> "hath never a child
> To honor before the rest."

She has one form of Baptism for the heir of kingdoms and for the poor man's child. She has the same office for Confirmation, and the hands of the Bishop which are laid on the heads of the rich and educated are not too good for the ignorant and poor. She ministers the same bread and the same cup to all of us. She says the same prayers for us when we are sick, and commits us with the same words to the common dust from which we sprang. In the house of God, as in "the house appointed for all living, the rich and the poor meet together, and the Lord is the Maker of them all."

The object of a religious service at the burial of the dead is two-fold:

1. Its design is, in the first place, to notice the event; to recognize it in its true character, as seen from a religious point of view; to give expression to the feeling it awakens in those who are affected by it, and which craves expression. This is all we can say of many observances which have no immediate practical effect, which

do not change facts at all, that they express something in us which craves expression. We are not satisfied to pass by great incidents in our lives and take no notice of them. It is a law of our nature that every inward feeling shall take outward shape and form. And so friendship has its clasping hand, and joy its melodies, and sorrow its tears—unsubstantial things, we know, mere shadows, yet we would not do without them. Unsubstantial, too, and unproductive of tangible results, is the ringing of bells, and the firing of guns, and the raising of flags, in times of national rejoicing; and the lowering of flags, and the tolling of bells, and the minute guns, which tell of national sorrow. Who is content to let occasions like these pass in silence by? They stir and express a feeling in all our hearts which craves expression, and if it is deep and solemn enough, we observe thanksgiving or fasting days in church for them; we bring these great events which move us so into the presence of God. We lift them out of their more present and obvious relations, which are sufficiently covered by the newspapers and by our common talk about them, up to that higher level of thought and feeling on which we walk with God.

Just this is one object of a burial service, in every instance—*to recognize the hand of God.*

2. But there is something to be effected more than this—more directly personal and practical,

as we use the word "practical"—in the comfort and consolation of those that mourn. Not simply to recognize the event as ordered by Divine providence, but to seek for and to find strength and support under it from the fulness of Divine grace. Probably the least religious of mourners is not without some recognition of this aspect of the service in which he is engaged.

And now I think we are safe in saying that no service which leaves our natural feeling out of the account, and directs itself simply to the presentation of such religious consideration as may utterly override and silence our natural grief, can ever carry the comfort that God intends. Have you never been met, in the first bitterness of grief, by the rigid, ungenial, unsympathetic pietism that tells you it is a sin to grieve, that the affliction is not so great as you deserve— which is true, of course; that you ought to be resigned—which is also true; that it is wholesome discipline and designed to do you good, all which is very true indeed, but which in the way it is presented, you resent and rebel against as if it were an utter falsehood? It is not that all these religious considerations are not true, it is that they are so placed and timed as to be, not in sympathy with, but in direct antagonism to the natural feeling of the hour. And therefore they do not soften the heart so much as harden and embitter it. "Light is good for the eyes, and a pleasant thing it is to behold the sun," but the sunlight flashed in suddenly on the dilated and sensitive pupil gives pain rather than pleasure. So sometimes an inconsiderate and unsympathetic mode of urging what are indeed and most truly the "consolations of religion" upon the heart that is darkened with sorrow, will rather shut it up altogether against the light. It will not open and expand, and look up into the face of God, but will close in sullenness upon its grief. Job's friends comforted him by their silence, but when they opened their mouths to interpret his sorrows, they only rasped and embittered him.

There is no greater untruth to the human nature and the religion that have been made for each other than to set them in violent antagonism. This is what sin does, in the interest, as it pretends, of human nature; let not the error be imitated on the other side, and nature be violated in the interest of religion. Human nature should not be told, in the first hour of a great grief, that it must not go down into the vale of sorrow, but rather to go down and through it into faith, and hope, and joy. From sunshine into shadow, and from shadow into sunshine again—this is the course of human experience, and sometimes the light and the shadow mingle strangely. For "joy and sorrow," it has been said, "are not enemies, but companionable and loving."

THE BURIAL SERVICE.

The key-note of the whole Burial Service is struck in the opening sentences. They speak of faith, and patience, and thanksgiving. They open with those words which are essentially Christian words—words in which Christ draws to Himself the faith and trust of His people—"I am the Resurrection and the Life."

The second passage is that from the book of Job, in which the patriarch rises up from the midst of his affliction, and out of all the doubt and uncertainty into which he is plunged by the mystery of God's dealings with him, and affirms and re-affirms his trust in God: many things I do not know—much there is which I cannot understand—but this *I know,* "that my Redeemer liveth," that He liveth Who shall vindicate me, standing at the latter day upon the earth. Yes, He shall appear for me, I shall see Him; shall see Him for myself, in my own person. I shall not lose myself in the general mass of being, mine eye shall behold Him, notwithstanding the dissolutions of death, and the corruptions of the grave.

And then there is that merging of grief in the joy of hope and trust which is expressed by the third of the opening sentences. We come into the world with nothing; one thing and another cleaves to us as we pass along, but they drop away from us, no matter how we loved them, and we pass out of the world naked as when we entered it. It was the Lord that gave, the Lord hath taken away. What then? Do we murmur? Nay, but we give thanks. In the hope of a resurrection, in the confidence of a righteous judgment, we say, "Blessed be the name of the Lord !"

After these sentences comes the Burial Psalm. Its burden is the shortness and uncertainty of human life. It takes up and gives expression to the sorrow of the hour. It is full of the mystery of death, and the greater mystery of life— vanity and shadow, labor and sorrow, disquietude and tears. There is no logical order of thought in this psalm—nothing but a certain sort of hopeless moaning, apathetic affirmation and reiteration of sorrowful truths, just as the heart turns its grief over and over, with a strange unmercifulness to itself, that it may lose not the least of its sorrow. It is just this correspondence with the facts of human experience that makes this Burial Service so comforting ; it does no violence to nature by repressing grief too soon, it rather leads it on, and relieves it by furnishing it with appropriate expression.

But merely to give expression to sorrow would very inadequately fulfil its purpose, and so, when the service has passed with us through the way of natural feeling, it carries us upward in its turn into the region of Christian faith, and opens out to us in the chapter from the epistle to the Corinthians, the thought of the resurrection of the dead. This wonderful chapter adduces first the proofs of Christ's Resurrection, and infers from that the certainty of our own. As surely as by our relation to the first Adam we are made subject to death, so surely does our resurrection from the dead result from our relation to Christ, the second Adam. If any one asks, honestly or cynically, "How are the dead raised up, and with what body do they come?" suggesting various difficulties in the way of the acceptance of the doctrine, these are disposed of by arguments drawn from the analogies of the natural world. This is the line taken by the Apostle in this chapter; but after all, we are moved not more by his logic than by the intensity of his own convictions, answering as they do to the cravings of our heart and of our intellect for light and knowledge of something beyond the grave. Somehow the thought of restoration of this loved form is conveyed over to the hearts of those who are sorrowing for its loss and ruin. We know not any more definitely after hearing it than we did before with what body the dead shall rise. That it is a spiritual body, more perfect, more glorious, more enduring, than this frail tenement of clay, and adapted to a higher sphere, all this we are somehow brought to feel, but what precisely the spiritual body is we cannot tell. All is vague, mysterious, yet comforting, reassuring. It almost seems an impertinence to stop and analyze the precise import of expressions which carry so much meaning to our hearts. The test of its truth to nature and to God is that it impresses its comforting convictions upon us when we are not in a logical mood, but when nature needs them most, and a loving Father most wants us to have them. Some one has well described this chapter as a being "like an anthem in the dark, great music and dim words."

The second half of the service, said at the brink of the grave, when grief breaks out again, is like the former. Down into the vale of sorrow again with the sad refrain, "Man that is born of a woman hath but a short time to live, and is full of misery," and with the dull thud of earth to earth upon the coffin-lid. And then up again into the view of the general resurrection. and the life of the world to come, and the rest from their labors of the dead who die in the Lord. And perhaps as remarkable as anything is the thanksgiving—for the idea of thanksgiving in a burial service is a striking, and unexpected, and altogether Christian idea: "We give Thee hearty thanks." That anything should be found to be thankful for at such a time can only be the result of Christian faith taking hold of this great grief, and lifting it up to its own higher level of thought and life.

How fully this service embodies the elements of strength and consolation which are contained in the Christian view of death! The assurance that we shall meet the same persons in the other world that we have known and loved in this; that they are now in a state of rest and hopeful waiting for our coming and the coming of the Lord; that they have gained infinitely by the change, and that our loss is only partial, and for a time ; all this, surely, contains the comfort that we need, and may raise us out of natural grief to something of the exultant feeling that finds expression in the Apostle's words: "O grave! where is thy victory? O death! where is thy sting?"

ADDRESS.

ALL SAINTS' DAY, SUNDAY, NOVEMBER 1ST, 1891.

ADDRESS

AT THE FIRST SERVICE IN THE THIRD PARISH CHURCH
OF ST. JOHN'S, STAMFORD, 1891.

By God's blessing on the work—for which, among other mercies, we thank and praise Him —we are entering on the use of this third parish church, for His worship, on All Saints' Day. Of all the days in the Christian year this is the happiest, most proper, most auspicious, for this event. It carries back our thought over nearly a century and a half to the men who founded this parish in times of hardness, poverty, and controversy (not to say persecution), now, happily, all but forgotten. The first church was five years in building, and when it was built was not larger than the chancel of this one in which we are assembled to-day. The family names of the builders of that church are represented in the contributors to this.

There has been a continuous record of Church life and growth through all these years. St. John's parish has a longer history than many of the Protestant denominations. It reaches back nearly half-way toward the Great Reformation itself. Its roots have struck deep into the soil of Stamford and the surrounding towns. Its fruits

ADDRESS.

have been seen in devout and useful lives of men and women, who have been as salt in the earth, and now do rest from their labors, while "their works do follow them." Let us remember them to-day with reverence and gratitude. And let their successors in the Christian ministry here especially remember the patience, the labors, the "perils by land and perils by water," the perils in the earlier days "among their own countrymen," endured honestly if mistakenly for conscience' sake, of Dr. Dibbler and his three successors in the rectorship, and follow them in so far as they have followed Christ.

And in one particular it is of special interest that this occasion should have fallen on this day of tender commemorations. Men and women whom we have known, who have passed away during my own term of ministry, are largely represented in the work which is consummated to-day. From John Ferguson, Eliza Leeds and her son, Charles W. Leeds, John Hubbard and others, we have received in trust fully one-third of the cost of the erection of this church, and the heirs of Moses Rogers dealt liberally with us in our purchase of the land for it four-and-twenty years ago. For nearly a quarter of a century the conception of this building has been in the minds and hearts of members of the congregation, and they whom I now recall have desired to enrich and beautify this temple of the Lord when it should be built. They did not leave what they have left in order to relieve their successors of responsibility, but to encourage and assist them that they might be generous to plan and execute. What they did has been an inspiration, and not an excuse. Like David of old, they made great store of provision, that we might build the more worthily. It was a sacred trust, and we have tried to fulfil it. If they know what has been done, we may be assured they approve our work. From their present point of view we may be sure they do not feel that we have done too much for the honor of God, or shown undue largeness in the enrichment of His house. Let us remember them to-day as our fellow-builders, and be grateful that we have been enabled to unite with them in devout and generous offerings for the work, and in that love for the habitation of God's house, and the place where His honor dwelleth, which alone could have prompted them to give and bequeath.

It is one of the many satisfactions to which the families of the parish are entitled in erecting a permanent and noble church, that it provides a fitting place for memorials of their departed. These grow and accumulate in such a building, and link the present with the past and the future. Already this natural sentiment has begun to find expression, and it is a wholesome and truly religious thought to fill this holy place of worship in the Church militant with family and

ADDRESS.

personal associations of those who are now worshippers in the Church Triumphant. It helps us to realize the communion of saints.

With these suggestions of the relation of the occasion to the day, let me now pass on to the natural line of thought which the entrance on the use of our new parish church suggests.

1. And first let me tell you what conception has been in my mind of the fitting manner in which to enter upon it. I explained to the Bishop, a few days since, why I had not asked him for the privilege and comfort of his presence with us on this occasion, and he entered most heartily into my feeling about it. The only form and manner which the Church provides for a ceremonial opening is the Form of Consecration of a church or chapel, and this we are not ready to use. But the presence of the Bishop at the opening service seems to most people to mean some sort of special dedication or consecration. As this church cannot now be duly consecrated, I have purposed to wait until the second of December, 1892, which will be the 150th anniversary of the founding of the parish. And it has never seemed to me either wise or fitting to anticipate, and so to weaken the significance of the solemn act of consecration by any half-way dedication or benediction. We ought honestly to recognize facts, and the fact is that this building is not yet ours to offer to God. And the Church prohibits the consecration of buildings

ADDRESS.

not fully paid for, because the offering would be, so far forth, an unreality.

I have therefore sought to make the occasion, as it were, a family occasion. We leave our chapel quietly, and quietly, but none the less joyfully and reverently, enter our parish church, and continue our stated worship here. I have invited as the preachers during the first month of its use clergymen who are of our parochial family by birth or residence, who have associations with us, which make their presence a homelike and interesting presence. And I feel very sure that your sentiment in this matter will correspond with mine, because it is a true and natural sentiment. Theirs is a home-coming—and theirs are home voices, yet not unknown abroad.

2. I desire also to recall and acknowledge the graceful hospitality of the Presbyterian Church here—who has sent me congratulations this morning—the hospitality which was extended to us on the first Sunday after the destruction of the old church, and the kindly offers of other churches here of similar accommodation. And we have been greatly indebted to St. Andrew's parish for the frequent use of its church for the celebration of the Occasional Offices of the Prayer Book at marriages and burials, and for the ample way in which it has been offered for any of our uses to which it was adequate.

But, indeed, we were singularly fortunate in

having a chapel of our own—indeed I may say *chapels,* for St. Luke's has served often for the Occasional Offices since it was opened six months ago—but especially a chapel here, on our own ground, readily adapted for the public worship of the congregation. It had some inconveniences, but then it was *our own,* and a very homelike place it was, and is. I am glad to have it derive some of that tenderness which attaches to the place where we worship statedly.

And there have been certain valuable results from our temporary occupancy of the chapel. In the first place, as the seats were free and unappropriated, it has brought people together, and made the congregation better acquainted. There were no exclusive rights; and while I think you might have "moved up" a little more readily at times, there has been a generous spirit of accommodation, and a good-humored acquiescence in crowding, and a general habit of neighborliness, which I hope will not be forgotten in the pews of the new church. And it was wonderful how prompt you all at once became in getting into church—a habit most desirable to be retained. And, moreover, I think you must all have been struck with the improvement in the responses, and with the general heartiness of the services. I was sorely discouraged at times, in the big old church, with the feebleness of the responding, and the listless way in which mostly you left the singing to the choir in the rear gallery. We are

not going to have any choir in the rear gallery—
the singers will now be where they will *lead*
the singing, but not monopolize it, or make a
"performance" of it. We shall hardly get back
to the old state of things, for everywhere our
church, and all churches, are growing in the
sense of worship. But I earnestly beg that you
will not be indifferent, or superior, or self-conscious, or afraid of the sound of your own voices,
but will render our inspiring liturgy as it should
be rendered by a large assembly of intelligent
and real worshippers.

3. And now, to come back to this building in
which we are assembled for the first time to-day,
what was it that we set out to do in its erection ?
The underlying motives and principles of our
undertaking were set forth in my sermon of February second, last year. On those principles we
have proceeded, I think, consistently. We have
done—what we set out to do. We set out to
build a church for the honor and worship of our
God—one which should adequately express the
religious sentiment, the convictions of duty
towards God, of a congregation not small nor
feeble; one which had long and honorable traditions, sufficient means (though perhaps not so
ample as some suppose), education in Church
principles; which had as a rule been responsive
to the claims of religion upon them; which was
placed in a position of influence and respect in a
large, and growing, and generally prosperous

ADDRESS.

community. This church was to be representative of the Christian religion in this place, inasmuch as its members are largely the representative men of the community, and cannot, and would not if they could, escape their consequent responsibility on its religious side. And we set out to build *a church,* not a meeting-house—a mere place of assembly—but a church which should embody the results of many centuries of growth in the conceptions of ecclesiastical architecture, every line of which should have its meaning and purpose. I am thankful that there are no modern architectural fads about this building; it is an Episcopal parish church, and cannot be mistaken for anything else. It is for the accommodation of a congregation, and it is also for their education, and the education of their children, and their children's children, in the idea that the worship of Almighty God is a thing of dignity, and cost, and sacrifice. It was not to be constructed according to any merely utilitarian standard—it was to be *a work of Christian art*—beauty, nobility, dignity, solemnity, were to be its characteristics. It was to be a *permanent* structure, solidly built, reasonably secure from fire and storm, an enduring monument of piety. Can any one give any good reason why the house of God should not be the best and noblest building in the town? Suppose the finest building in the town were a bank—what would be the story that fact would tell?

The Christian sentiment is, that the church should be the noblest, and we have desired to give expression to this Christian sentiment, *that what is offered and dedicated for God's service should be the best—*THE BEST.

There are two reasons for which the parish might conceivably come to be ashamed of itself when all is finished. The first is, *having undertaken more than it can do,* for that would not be honest. Mind I do not say "more than it can *easily* do." The second is, *having been satisfied to undertake less than it can do.* In such a matter as this, the former is the more excusable mistake, but we are bound to find just the point to which our ability extends, and *to come up to it.* The point at which generosity becomes extravagance, and the point where economy becomes meanness, are sometimes equally hard to fix, *but they are somewhere.* And people's judgment as to this point will be influenced by their general attitude towards religion, whether they think that anything is good enough for the church, or whether they think nothing is good enough for it. I think this church is mainly the legitimate outcome of a large faith, a large charity, a warm devotion to God and to whatever connects the human heart and life with God; that it is the work of men and women who have been willing to make exertions and sacrifices, to give and to give again, who have desired to realize an ideal which cannot be realized all at once, who

ADDRESS.

have desired to enrich and adorn the house of God—a reasonable ideal, a rational desire, if God and His belongings are indeed anything to them. Such people are not going to be content with what might merely "answer the purpose," as some might put it, like a Gothic shanty in a frontier town. For, what is, in reality the "purpose"? Not to build what *we* could get along with, as if we were just beginning, and had not a hundred and fifty years behind us, and many centuries before us. But, to honor our fathers' God and ours, by making His house beautiful, and His worship dignified, impressive, elevating; to put much into it so that we may get much out of it; to benefit the community by a signal assertion of the supreme place of the Christian religion in its life—this was the purpose this Church was designed to answer.

4. How far this high ideal has been realized you have now the opportunity to judge. I am glad to believe that what has been done is generally approved by the congregation. You gave what you have given—the departed givers gave what they did—to build something as worthy at least as this, and with the means at our disposal we have carried the building thus far towards its completion. There has been, in the progress of the work, little of the friction and few of the delays which so often mar the comfort and satisfaction of such enterprises. The designer, the contractors, and the representatives

ADDRESS.

of the parish, have worked in harmony. I cannot refrain from bearing testimony to the efficiency and truth, in all departments, with which the work has been carried on. And it is matter for great thankfulness, especially in the building of a church, when from first to last the work has been done without serious accident to life or limb. As one watches the workmen the marvel grows that it can be so.

This church is larger than the old one, but not unreasonably larger. That contained 730 sittings, of which about 130 were set apart as free. This contains about 600 sittings in pews, and has accommodation in the gallery and in chairs for about 250 free sittings in addition, making about 850 in all. This should be ample for a regular congregation. Few things are more deceptive than the number present in a public assembly. There is always much unoccupied space in a pewed church, unless the pew-holders are hospitable.

5. It was not the thought of your representatives in the work to complete the building at this time with tower and spire. That could not have been done without such large gifts from a very few as would make it *their* work and not the work of the congregation as a whole—a most undesirable result. And St. John's has never been under oppressive and compromising obligations to any man. There is no reason why it should be. It is a great satisfaction to

know that the response to the appeal for contributions has been so very general, that there have been so many small contributions as amounts go, though not always small as proportioned to ability. This means that most precious of all things—love, expressing itself in sacrifice. Our purpose was rather to do in the best and truest manner what was necessary and sufficient, and in doing that to build so worthily that what has been done should be an inspiration for the future to go on and complete the work in like manner. We have set the tone and measure. We might, of course, have taken even what had been left to us, and built a church adequate to the accommodation of the congregation, and made a very respectable building of it, too; and you might have invested *your* money at 5 per cent., and not have felt any strain or claim upon yourselves. Little interest in this work would you then have had. Nobody has much interest in what others do, even when he has the advantage of it. But this—it is never the sort of thing that a man regrets.

This same satisfaction is before us still, and before those who may follow us here. I believe the next generation of active parishioners, if we are willing to wait so long for the completion of the church, will thank us for the opportunity. But indeed after a few years you will be wanting the privilege for yourselves. Those who do the most are quite as likely to fall short of their own

ADDRESS.

desires as anybody, and desires ripen into purposes with time and opportunity. The present and the future members of the church may surely be trusted as much as the past to give and to bequeath.

6. Some disappointment—not enough, I am afraid—is felt that this is not to be what is generally known as *a free church*. The conception of a spiritual home for the community, in which no consideration of ability or willingness to support it is allowed to make any difference, but where the ministrations of religion are freely dispensed to all, is a generous and inspiriting one. There are other considerations, however, which are equally entitled to respect. I am not going into any discussion of the general question, but simply to state the controlling consideration which has decided the matter. It is just the consideration of *honesty*. It would not have been *honest* in the Vestry to incur obligations which they had no reasonable expectation of being able to fulfil. The chapel has for twenty-one months been a "free church," and it is found that the income under that system has not been adequate to meet the expenses. In the last six months it has been little more than half of what was needed. This indicates that the congregation as a whole is not ready for a change in its long-settled habit, and the habit generally of the old and established parishes. A free church implies an endowment which will cover

one-half the cost of maintaining it, or else such large assessments on a few persons that they practically dominate the church, which usually is a disadvantage. A parish sometimes becomes subservient to men of means for what they are expected to do for it. Mostly, they don't do what is expected; but the result is the same. We have no such endowment—at present not a penny of income from property. And we do not want to be under obligations. The congregation is able to support the church, and it evidently prefers to support it mainly by that voluntary and proportionate system which is known as the pew-renting system. This is the common-sense of our actual situation.

At the same time the generous free church sentiment and principle—for it is not *mere* sentiment—finds such expression as the circumstances of the parish, and its situation in just this sort of community, makes appropriate. In the three churches and chapels which the parish sustains, are 1200 sittings, 600 of which are absolutely free and unappropriated. Nobody who is likely to want to worship in our church in Stamford, either occasionally or regularly, need stay away for want of room. In this church there is room for 250 free sittings, in St. Luke's Chapel there are upwards of 250 more, and in Emmanuel Church another hundred. And in this parish church seats are assigned to regular contributors under the envelope system without reference to the amount of their contributions, but simply to the fact that they are parishioners. I think sometimes that some reminder is needed that pew-holders, who are the regular attendants and supporters of the church have their rights as well as others who are not. One of them, which they are not slow to exercise, is the right to the opportunity of being courteous and hospitable with unoccupied spaces after seating their own families, who have the first claim to consideration. It appears to me that an adjustment has been reached which duly recognizes a true sentiment without sacrificing practical wisdom to it, which secures business honesty in the administration of church finance, and which is the best we can do under the circumstances. I trust the day may come when we can do better. It will come when we have an endowment of $100,000. In the meantime it seems likely that the revenue from pews and sittings will meet the ordinary requirements for maintaining the church, and the parochial collections will be so much toward the interest on our indebtedness for the building until that indebtedness is removed.

I have said enough about the situation. It only remains that I should voice your thankfulness for the realization of a long hope, your appreciation of the labors—not few nor small—of those who have had the special charge of this work, your admiration of its excellence—the

ADDRESS.

dignity, fitness, and beauty of this church; and that I should bid you welcome to its use for worship on this tender and inspiring day. I call upon you to be generous and hospitable in welcoming strangers and fellow citizens to your privileges. I call you to hearty and worthy worship of your God in this, His holy temple. And let no holy and gracious activities in our own community be impaired; our charities, especially our Church House and Hospital work, and our parochial missions, should find invigoration, and not atrophy, from our worship here. And sorry, indeed, will it be if we relax our interest in the general missions and charities of our Church throughout the land. Let this edifice on which we enter to-day be—not the costly mausoleum of a dead church—but the warm and happy home of a living, the centre of its loving activities for man, and of its inspiring and elevating worship of God.

www.ingramcontent.com/pod-product-compliance
Lightning Source LLC
Chambersburg PA
CBHW031903220426
43663CB00006B/740